POLICE
RANGE ROVERS

A FIFTY YEAR STORY

PETER HALL

Grosvenor House
Publishing Limited

This book is published by
Grosvenor House Publishing Ltd
Link House
140 The Broadway, Tolworth, Surrey, KT6 7HT.
www.grosvenorhousepublishing.co.uk

A CIP record for this book
is available from the British Library

ISBN 978-1-83975-271-1

CONTENTS

INTRODUCTION

My interest in Range Rovers began in the summer of 1971 when I was six and my Dad gave me a bronze coloured Dinky Toy model of one and a copy of the first sales brochure. These items, which I treasured for many years, were the beginning of an interest which continues, unabated, to the present day. I joined the Kent County Constabulary in 1986 and was posted to Margate. The force had used Range Rovers for many years and I remember seeing C927 SMV, the last Kent Traffic Range Rover, when I was pounding the beat, policing the 1987 Scooter Rally. Sadly, the Range Rovers had gone by the time I joined Traffic and it was not until 1995 that I drove my first Police Range Rover. This was one of the Kent Incident Command Vehicles (ICVs); four top of the range Vogue LSEs converted for Police use. I became heavily involved in the ICV project, my last work being to introduce the 'second generation' ICVs (three T registered P38 models) into service in 1999. It was whilst I was working on the ICV project that I started to research and write The Police Range Rover Handbook which was published in 1998 by British Bus Publishing Ltd.

I retired from the Police in 2016 and I assumed that The Police Range Rover Handbook had long been forgotten and that there was little interest in Police Range Rovers. I was proved to be very wrong on both counts and it was clear that, with large numbers of retired officers and Police vehicle enthusiasts taking an active part in social media, there was a huge amount of previously unseen photographs and great sources of new information available. Now, as in 1998, I found myself relying a great deal on the memories of serving and retired officers and their personal photographs. The internet and social media have enabled me to add previously unrecorded Police Range Rovers and also correct a number of errors in the original book. In addition, the Police

Range Rover Handbook was written as the last Range Rover Classics were in service and the first P38 Range Rovers were beginning to join the ranks of UK Police vehicles. Since then, there have been two 'new' Range Rovers; the L322 in 2002 and the L405 in 2012 and both have seen use by UK Police forces.

The majority of the photographs in this book are not professional products, many being just 'happy snaps', taken by whatever cameras officers or Police vehicle enthusiasts had at the time; certainly, long before digital cameras or the mobile phone age. Whilst many are superb quality, some are not but I have included them because they are unique; the only record of vehicles (and an important part of UK Police history) long gone. That said, I have been lucky to receive a huge number of outstanding photos from some really good photographers and I am very grateful for their help. I have tried very hard to locate the original photographer; a task made a lot harder by many copies of the same photograph being widely circulated on the internet. I apologise in advance if any photographs are inaccurately credited.

The members of a number of retired Police and Police vehicle social media groups have been incredibly helpful, supplying photographs and information unobtainable from anywhere else. They are far too numerous to mention individually but I thank them all for their help and for putting up with my repetitive requests for information and photographs.

This book is dedicated to Traffic officers who, since 1971, have used and abused, loved and loathed the Range Rover during the course of their often-dangerous duties.

PHOTO 1 – The Dinky Toy model Range Rover that started it all (Author's collection)

PHOTO 2 – PC 1740 Albert Hover of the Kent County Constabulary, pictured with 'his' Range Rover, GKJ 966L, at the Police Post, M2 Services, Farthing Corner, in 1973 (Albert Hover)

PHOTO 3 – Sgt 1039 Norman Woollons of Humberside Police, pictured with 'his' Range Rover, C183 CAG, at Millington in the Yorkshire Wolds, in 1986 (Wayne York via Norman Woollons)

PHOTO 4 – PC 8007 Peter Hall of the Kent County Constabulary, pictured with 'his' Range Rover, L925 WCD, at the Force Tactical Team, Nackington, near Canterbury, in 1998 (Author)

PHOTO 5 – PC 9990 Alan Black of the Police Service of Northern Ireland, pictured with 'his' Range Rover, UCZ 7324, at the Parliament Buildings, Stormont, near Belfast, in 2008 (Alan Black)

PHOTO 6 – Two Greater Manchester Range Rovers and West Yorkshire's H78 SWX meet in suitably Pennine Hills weather during the Winter of 1990 / 1991. The photo was taken on the A672, just off Junction 22 of the M62 motorway. The crews are (left to right): The late PC Dennis Harrison (GMP), West Yorkshire PC, PC Bob Finegan (GMP) and West Yorkshire PC (Bob Finegan)

PHOTO 7 – The way it was; 'Range Rover Heaven', Birch Services on the M62 motorway (Steve Pearson)

CHAPTER 1

RANGE ROVER – A CAR FOR ALL REASONS

Love 'em or loathe 'em

The launch of the Range Rover on 17th June 1970 opened an entirely new chapter in motoring; there had never been anything quite like it before. Advertised at the launch as 'A Car For All Reasons', the Range Rover offered a top speed in excess of 100 mph, a towing capacity of 3.5 tons, spacious accommodation for five people, hydraulic disc brakes on all wheels, and a ground breaking four speed, dual range, permanent four-wheel drive gearbox. All of these features, common enough now, were almost unique in 1970 when the average family saloon was incapable of reaching 100 mph.

To the Police of 1970, four-wheel drive vehicles would have meant Land Rovers which had been in service with many forces for years. Whilst the Land Rovers were excellent for rural patrol work, as motorway patrol vehicles they were hopeless. What was remarkable about the Range Rover was that, for the first time, there was a vehicle with good performance (i.e. it could sustain 100 mph), the comfort of a car and the towing and off-road capability of a Land Rover. It was no surprise that the Police were so impressed with the Range Rover, especially after W.R. Taylor of 'Police Review' magazine tested an early example and wrote: 'Unsurpassed versatility is perhaps the shortest and most complete summing up that could be made about the Range Rover. Few vehicles have caused such a stir in Police circles when the details were only rumoured and now that the full specification is available for all to see, the stir is even greater – and with just cause. In all the years I have been road testing vehicles I have never come across such a universally acceptable, or ready made, Police vehicle as the Range Rover. The Range Rover is a difficult vehicle to fault from any point of view and in spite of its apparent size, it can be got through traffic quicker than most vehicles due to the excellence of the driver's view plus the acceleration that permits overtakes to be snatched'.

There is not, and never has been, a national policy for buying Police vehicles in the United Kingdom (UK). The various forces have always been able to make their own decisions when buying their vehicles and this has generally been the best option as the needs of the forces differ so greatly. Some forces, for example, would have no use whatsoever for four-wheel drive vehicles, whilst others in rural areas might consider them to be essential. The same would apply to almost every other type of Police vehicle, including the high-performance motorway patrol vehicles used by Traffic / Roads Policing Divisions.

The Police vehicle market is obviously lucrative and prestigious for vehicle manufacturers and over the years many have done their best conquer it. Some have even gone to the expense of developing Police concept vehicles, intending them to be the perfect Police vehicle but few, if any, have been successful. Despite this, there are vehicles which have won almost universal approval as Traffic patrol cars; the Rover P6 3500 (1968 – 1977), the Vauxhall Senator Mark 2 ('B') 3.0 24v (1989 – 1993) and the Volvo V70 T5 estate (1996 – 2016), for example. In recent years, the Police vehicle market in terms of Traffic (now usually called 'Roads Policing') vehicles has been almost completely dominated by BMW with their 5 Series Touring (estate) and X5 four-wheel drive vehicles, both almost certain to become the classic Police vehicles of their time.

Police vehicles, especially the higher performance Traffic vehicles, are generally well driven and well maintained, but the life they lead is as hard as it could be, most travelling in excess of 50,000 miles a year, often at very high speed and loaded with a great deal of emergency equipment. To survive in that environment is a real test of any manufacturer's ability and many otherwise superb vehicles are simply not able to cope with the punishment of Police work. Those that do survive are all remarkable vehicles and the Range Rover is most definitely one of them.

In 1970 the Range Rover was all conquering but as the performance of family saloons increased and other, often better, vehicles became available, the Range Rover began to lose its tremendous advantages over its rivals and there was a real danger that it would fall from favour with the Police. Another reason for the potential fall was the sometimes appalling reliability of the early vehicles; something that the forces suffered well into the 21st century. Officers who drove the Range Rover in Police service tell of amazing feats such as pulling heavily laden articulated goods vehicles off the motorway and driving in blizzard conditions that would have defeated any other vehicle. They also tell of rusting tailgates falling off whilst on patrol and one Fleet Manager described the Range Rover as 'the best thing I ever got rid of'; yet another told of a gearbox which failed as the brand new Range Rover was being driven into the workshops to be marked and equipped for service. Many Police Range Rovers covered well over 150,000 miles with few if any problems, but far too many suffered from engine, gearbox and latterly electronic air suspension problems; all problems which continued in 2002 when the first L322 Range Rovers entered Police service.

In the 1980s and 1990s, the Range Rover began to climb ever upwards, both in luxury and in cost. Whilst some of the equipment fitted was undoubtedly useful to the Police, with force budgets coming under ever increasing scrutiny, it was becoming increasingly difficult to justify the expense of the Range Rover and the Police began to look seriously at other vehicles.

The Competition

Despite there being no national policy in the UK for buying Police vehicles there was, for many years, a probably unwritten but fairly rigidly adhered to policy, of 'Buy British'. There were always exceptions to the rule however, and Hampshire was the first UK Police force to buy a foreign vehicle when they bought their first Volvo 121 Amazon estate car in June 1965. The Range Rover was fairly safe from any competition until the Isuzu Trooper was launched in the UK in 1987 (with a five door version arriving in January 1988). Leicestershire was the first of several forces to buy the Trooper or the Monterey, the Vauxhall-badged version of it. Other foreign competitors for the Range Rover over the years have included the Jeep Cherokee, the Mercedes G Wagen and ML320, the Mitsubishi Shogun and the Toyota Land Cruiser. The move away from the Range Rover was not always a happy or successful one, however, and there were forces that regretted it, with some quickly returning to using Range Rovers.

The biggest threat to the Range Rover's almost thirty year dominance of Britain's motorways began in 1999 when BMW launched the X5 four-wheel drive vehicle. Developed when BMW owned Land Rover, the X5 benefitted from Land Rover technology whilst featuring the engine and electronics of the BMW 5 series cars. The 3.0 litre M57 diesel engine was reliable and certainly powerful enough for Police use. The engine, equipment levels and impressive reliability, combined with a very skilful marketing campaign, quickly made the X5 the vehicle of choice in the Traffic and Armed Response Vehicle role for almost every UK Police force.

Once again Hampshire, always an innovative force in terms of the vehicles they used, led the way with HN02 UDK, the first Police BMW X5 in the UK. The vehicle was registered on 18th June 2002, replacing an S registered P38 Range Rover which had been destroyed by vandals in a fire. HN02 UDK was given the callsign Mike Charlie 1, allocated to PC Steve Woodward and, based at the Traffic garage at Cosham near Portsmouth, it spent its Police service patrolling the M27, M275 motorways and the A3(M).

Staying with Land Rover

Despite the strong competition and despite the problems with reliability, the Range Rover was still the vehicle of choice for many UK Police forces; there simply was nothing better. The last years of Range Rover Classic production (1994 / 1995 and 1995 / 1996, with M and N registrations respectively) saw large purchases by some of the major Police fleets, notably Greater Manchester who registered eleven Classics in May and June 1995, and the Metropolitan Police in London.

The P38 Range Rover was launched in September 1994 and Land Rover made sure that at least six of the early vehicles were Police demonstrators. The company was quick off the mark with the vehicles being registered in October 1994 and M752 CVC and M774 CVC on loan to the Central Motorway Police Group in the West Midlands the same month. Several forces made early purchases of the P38 Range Rover; there were at least fifteen N registered vehicles across seven forces and at least twenty seven P registered vehicles across eight forces. It was a hopeful start but sadly there were still problems with reliability (often centred on the air suspension) and towards the end of the P38 Range Rover's production run, the BMW X5 was launched. Nevertheless, at least eighteen forces went on the buy the P38 Range Rover and it was still a common enough sight on UK motorways.

The L322 Range Rover was launched in February 2002 and was way ahead of the P38 in terms of build quality and reliability; not that the L322 was entirely trouble free. By 2002, however, BMW was starting to seriously market the X5 to the Police and the Series II Discovery was becoming more popular than the Range Rover with UK forces (see below). Both of these factors meant decreasing sales of the Range Rover to the Police but there was another very important factor at this time; the introduction of civilian Highways Agency Traffic Officers (HATOs) and the inevitable reduction in numbers of Police Traffic officers which followed. The HATOs began working alongside Police Officers in West Midlands in

April 2004 and by July 2006 they covered the whole motorway network in England. Their role is to patrol and respond to motorway incidents (but not to police them) and they often use the same types of four-wheel drive vehicles as their Police predecessors. In April 2015, the Highways Agency became Highways England and the HATOs became HETOs. Their role, however, remains unchanged and they are a familiar sight on England's motorways; often more familiar than Police patrols.

The Land Rover Discovery was launched in September 1989 but with a three door body and the 200 Tdi diesel engine, it did not offer the required performance for motorway work; the Discovery in its early years was not a popular option for Police Traffic Divisions. The launch of the five door Discovery in October 1990 did improve the situation slightly but the forces that bought the 200 Tdi Discovery for motorway work almost universally regretted the purchase; Hampshire officers called them 'Tractors' and Kent officers called them 'Sheds', for example. The launch of the Series II Discovery in November 1998 changed the situation dramatically. The Series II was an almost completely new vehicle, centred on two outstanding engines; the Td5 diesel and the latest 'Thor' version of the Rover V8 petrol engine. The Discovery improved at just the right time to attract UK Police forces and several forces that had used Range Rovers for years went on to buy the Series II Discovery (1998 – 2004), Discovery 3 (2004 – 2009), Discovery 4 (2009 – 2016) and Discovery 5 (2016 onwards).

The L405 Range Rover was launched at the Paris Motor Show in September 2012 and whilst it is undoubtedly a world beating vehicle, it is not really a vehicle for the Police in the UK. With the all-conquering BMW X5 and other perfectly acceptable Land Rover products available, it becomes increasingly difficult to justify the expense of the latest Range Rover. That said, at the time of writing, the Police Range Rover lives on, in service with the Metropolitan Police who have four L405 Range Rovers, marked in the 'Battenburg' livery and often seen at high profile events in London.

So, fifty years on from the launch of the Range Rover, they are still used by the UK Police; albeit in very small numbers. It has been a long and not always easy journey but despite this, the earliest vehicles are remembered, usually with a degree of fondness, by veteran Traffic officers, one of whom said of the Range Rover; 'Love 'em or loathe 'em, they were a superb special role vehicle'.

PHOTO 1 – G41 VJF, one of Leicestershire's Isuzu Troopers dating from August 1989 (Chris Taylor)

PHOTO 2 – One of the Greater Manchester Police Mercedes ML320s, MT02 BEY, registered in July 2002 (Maurice Kime)

PHOTO 3 – Hampshire's HN02 UDK, the first UK Police BMW X5 (Steve Woodward)

PHOTO 4 – WX17 HYY, a Wiltshire BMW X5, registered on 1st August 2017 (Steve Pearson)

PHOTO 5 – Strathclyde's H348 FAC, a Discovery V8i based at the Glasgow Motorway Unit. It replaced B875 BGA, Strathclyde's last three door Range Rover, and was sold in 1999 having covered 228,508 miles (Jim Burns)

PHOTO 6 – T209 LLH, the first Police Series II Discovery. The vehicle, a Td5 model, was registered by the Metropolitan Police on 20th July 1999 and based at London's Heathrow Airport (Andy Bardsley)

PHOTO 7 – AY18 FEH, a joint Norfolk / Suffolk Discovery powered by the 3.0 litre V6 diesel engine (Steve Pearson)

PHOTO 8 – A Highways England Discovery (Shaun Henderson)

CHAPTER 2

INTO SERVICE

The 'Midland Links' & the first demonstrators

In 1958 the Department of Transport commenced the Midland Links Motorway Project. This ambitious plan was designed to link the major motorways of England, using Birmingham as a central hub. The M6 motorway was to be extended south from Junction 13 at Dunston in Staffordshire to Ray Hall at West Bromwich where it would meet the extended M5. The M6 was also to be extended east, finally meeting the M1 at Catthorpe in Leicestershire. At the same time, the City of Birmingham was to construct to A38(M) Aston Expressway, linking the city centre with the M6. The 'Midland Links' included the famous 'Spaghetti Junction'; more accurately Junction 6 of the M6 or the Gravelly Hill Interchange, which linked the M6 to the A38(M).

By 1968 construction was well under way and the project to police the Midland Links began in May of that year. The new motorway system passed through five Police force areas; Birmingham City, Staffordshire, Warwickshire & Coventry, West Mercia and West Midlands and to police it effectively would take unprecedented cooperation between the forces. The task of organising the joint Police group fell to Superintendent W.R. Morris who at that time commanded the Birmingham City Police Traffic Division. 'Motorway' Morris, as he became known, was a man of exceptionally high standards who demanded the very best from his officers and who did not suffer fools at all. From the outset he knew that the task of policing the new motorway network would be extremely demanding and the standards that he set would serve the unit well for many years. In addition to organising the Police group, Supt Morris was also tasked with planning a single control centre to control to entire 43.25 miles of motorway.

A site was chosen at Perry Barr, next to the M6 in north Birmingham, and the control centre was built there. It was very advanced for its time, including features such as Close Circuit Television cameras covering the whole network and overhead gantries with information signs on them. The location of the centre, which also housed a Traffic garage, was well chosen as it could also control the planned southern motorway (which eventually became the M42).

With the busy, often elevated, motorways came a need for a new type of Police vehicle. The Jaguar XJ 4.2s then in service were excellent for enforcement but could not remove obstructions like cars and heavy good vehicles from the carriageway. West Midlands Police had used Land Rovers in the past and it was suggested that a 'high speed' Land Rover would be ideal for the new motorway role. With this in mind, Supt Morris approached the British Leyland Motor Corporation (which owned Rover) to see if such a vehicle was available or if one could be developed for Police use.

Coincidentally, at this time the Rover New Vehicle Projects Department was working on the Range Rover, under the leadership of C.S 'Spen' King. Two Engineering Prototypes had already been built and the team knew that the Range Rover was exactly what the Police were looking for. At a meeting on 18th December 1968 between the New Vehicle Projects Department and the Sales Department, it was decided that the Police would be offered the Range Rover in advance of the official launch, then scheduled for the Geneva Motor Show in March 1970. It is not known if the Police ever trialled a prototype Range Rover, but this may well have been the case as they were certainly demonstrated to senior officers. The Range Rover was eventually launched on 17th June 1970 and sales to the public began in September.

The Range Rover was an instant success with the public but Rover's Home Sales Department had not forgotten the Police as one of the earliest production vehicles became the first Police demonstrator. Chassis number 35500082A (the 82nd Range Rover to be built and fitted with V8 engine number 12) was registered as PXC 575J on 14th September 1970. The vehicle was marked with the usual Police red stripes on the sides and it was fitted a single blue light and 'Police' sign on the roof, a flashing 'Police' sign on the bonnet and a sign on the rear which could read either 'Stop' or 'Accident'. PXC 575J was, therefore, an almost standard Range Rover and it was trialled by a number of UK Police forces over the next few years; most of them simply could not wait to get their hands on the new vehicle.

At almost the same time as PXC 575J began its journey around the UK, a Blackpool based company called Radiotelecommunications, working in conjunction with Rover, unveiled the 'Emergency Services' Range Rover at the London Commercial Motor Show, held on 26th September 1970. The vehicle, unregistered but known as the 'Vigilant', was a radical concept vehicle fitted with a large roof fairing housing a 'Police' sign and two spot lights. It was also fitted with a capstan winch, hidden behind the grille, and two large emergency equipment lockers where the rear windows would normally be. Radical and well thought out the Vigilant may have been, it was not as good as the standard Range Rover and this, combined with the fact that the equipment lockers actually made it more difficult to access equipment and also seriously reduced visibility, meant that the vehicle was never adopted by any Police force.

The first Police Range Rovers

Orders for the Range Rover far exceeded production in the autumn of 1970 and the Police had to wait like everyone else. Following the early contact by Supt Morris, the Midland Links Motorway Police Group placed the first order for Police Range Rovers, ordering six vehicles. It soon became apparent, however, that the motorways would not open until early 1971 and also that Rover was struggling to provide the fleet of six vehicles. Thus, it fell to Lincolnshire, a force that only ordered two vehicles, to be the first force to use the Range Rover. Cheshire, the Midland Links and Northamptonshire quickly followed and so the Police Range Rover story began.

The first Police Range Rovers were J registered (August 1970 – July 1971):

- Lincolnshire: VFW 918J and VFW 919J, registered on 29th January 1971
- Cheshire: STU 699J to STU 703J, registered on 1st February 1971
- Northamptonshire: YBD 579J, YNV 271J and YNV 272J, registered on 4th February 1971
- Midland Links: XOG 1J to XOG 6J, registered on 26th March 1971
- North Yorkshire: VPY 682J, registered on 1st April 1971, VPY 683J and VPY 684J, registered on 24th April 1971
- Warwickshire: CNX 802J, registered on 20th May 1971, and CUE 391J, registered on 26th May 1971
- Lancashire: FTC 262J and FTC 263J, registered on 10th June 1971
- Kent: YKN 631J, registered on 17th June 1971
- Durham: NPT 371J, registered in June 1971
- Hertfordshire: WNK 418J, registered in July 1971

The Chief Constable of Northamptonshire, Mr J.H. Gott, MBE, GM, QPM, BA, (who was also a keen motorsport competitor) summed up the Range Rover's entry into Police service: 'One vehicle which has so far lived up to its promise is the Range Rover which is now in service with my force for motorway patrol. For this specialised role I felt the patrol car should be a high performance, comfortable load carrier and have the capability of keeping going when other vehicles were defeated by the conditions...It easily carries the large amount of special equipment necessary to assist the crew in dealing with the serious accidents which occur all too frequently on motorways and with its outstanding ground clearance is a real cross country vehicle, literally able to climb motorway banks if necessary. For a car of its size and shape the performance is outstanding, with maximum speed in the high nineties, acceleration to match and very good handling.'

PHOTO 1 – Supt W.R. 'Motorway' Morris of the Birmingham City Police, photographed when he had been promoted to the rank of Chief Superintendent (Mrs Lorraine Morris)

PHOTO 2 – PXC 575J, the first Police Range Rover demonstrator, photographed in February 1971 on farmland owned by Rover (BMIHT)

PHOTO 3 – The 'Vigilant' Police concept vehicle, dating from September 1970 (Author's collection)

PHOTO 4 – Lincolnshire's VFW 918J and VFW 919J, the first Police Range Rovers, photographed when they entered service in 1971 (Lincolnshire Police)

PHOTO 5 – Cheshire's STU 699J (via Karl Dillon)

PHOTO 6 – Northamptonshire's first three Range Rovers at the official handover in March 1971 at Rothersthorpe (now Northampton) Services on the M1 motorway (John Mayes)

PHOTO 7 – A rare colour photograph of West Midlands' XOG 6J (Alan Matthews collection)

PHOTO 8 – North Yorkshire's VPY 682J shown at the Traffic Garage at Racecourse Lane, Northallerton (via Karl Dillon)

CHAPTER 3

'POLICE SPEC'

Early Days

Following the success of the first Police Range Rover demonstrator and the lack of interest that UK Police forces had shown in the 'Vigilant' concept vehicle, it was obvious to Rover that the standard Range Rover was perfect for Police use with few, if any, modifications. The very earliest Police Range Rovers were almost certainly standard civilian models, with the Police equipment being added by the forces, but it was clear that there were some basic requirements common to every force. These requirements became the basis of the Police Specification ('Police Spec') throughout the production life of the Range Rover Classic and continued with the later Police Range Rover models.

The earliest Police Specification was featured in the first Police Range Rover sales brochure (Rover reference 838 / 5.72), published in May 1972. The brochure featured Warwickshire's two J registered Range Rovers with K suffixes airbrushed onto the photographs and the early Police Specification was listed as:

- 20 ACR, 60A alternator (battery sensed)
- Split charge facility for radio communications
- Electrical harness for roof auxiliaries
- Additional CA9 battery, clamps and cables
- Battery condition meter (switches to sense vehicle or auxiliary battery)
- Switch panel: six switches of the three position (Off / 1/ 2) type providing control of up to 12 functions; two warning lights (red and blue); fusebox giving protection for each switch

- Additional interior light mounted in rear roof
- Calibrated speedometer in nacelle, mounted in dash centre with drive to calibrated speedometer only; or with 'split drive' to retain operation of normal speedometer

By October 1974, 'Police Spec' had been updated and was listed in the latest brochure (Rover reference RT 901 / 10.74):

- Lucas 60A 20 ACR alternator
- 80 – 0 – 80 ammeter
- Heavy duty 70Ah battery

Optional

- Split charge facility with additional 80 – 0 – 80 ammeter
- Additional 70Ah battery
- Switch panel with six rocker switches, red and blue warning lights and additional fusebox
- Auxiliary wiring harness
- Additional interior light mounted in rear roof
- Calibrated speedometer mounted in nacelle in dash centre (standard speedometer operative or inoperative as specified)
- Observers rear view mirror
- Butler flexilite
- Equipment trays
- Two roof mounted spotlights (SL130 type)
- Fiamm air horns

Optional Equipment (factory or dealer fitted as appropriate)

- Laminated windscreen
- Sundym glass
- Tow bar and hook assembly
- Front mounted winches – 3000lb pull capstan; 50000lb pull electric

Fleetline

In the early 1980s, as the Range Rover began its climb to ever increasing luxury and its competitors improved, there was a real danger that the major fleet users, especially the Police, would abandon it. Determined to keep this important market, Land Rover Ltd introduced the Range Rover Fleetline in June 1981. This model, which the Police purchased in fairly large numbers, was a two door model with most of the 'luxury' items deleted. The specification included:

- Vinyl seat facings
- Vinyl spare wheel and tool cover
- Rubber floor mats
- No head restraints
- No power assisted steering
- No radio aerial or door mounted speakers
- No under bonnet inspection lamps

By 1984 / 85 most Police forces had followed the civilian trend and started buying the four door Range Rover. The need for the Fleetline was rapidly diminishing and so production ceased. One of the last Range Rover price lists to feature the Fleetline was issued on 14th January 1985 (the vehicle cost £13,631.90) and production of it had almost certainly ceased by October 1985 when the fuel injected Range Rover was introduced. The Police then found themselves back in the mainstream Range Rover market, although 'Police Spec' was still being offered, with a later version being listed in the April 1989 Range Rover Parts Catalogue (covering vehicles up to October 1985):

Normal extras incorporated

£1595	Heated backlight with clear glass
£1637	Electrical requirements for heated rear screen, 25 ACR alternator 60 amp or Series 'A' 65 amp
£6257	Splash shields and caliper for rear brakes

Special Features

Calibrated speedometer centrally mounted in separate binnacle,
both calibrated and vehicle speedometers are in operation
Michelin tyres only to be fitted, 205 x 16 Radial Mud and Snow
Two heavy duty batteries (one for vehicle, one auxiliary)
Change-over switch for battery condition meter (Voltmeter basic
fitment on current models)
Auxiliary switch panel and warning lights at dash centre
Fuse box mounted adjacent to terminal bracket on LH valance for
auxiliary split charging system
Map reading lamp
Electrical cables and harnesses to suit auxiliary equipment
Existing speaker grille modified to accommodate speedometer
cable
Observer's rear-view mirror
Pulley for water pump with ratio of 0.88:1 ratio to crankshaft
Untrimmed steering wheel
Palomino vinyl lower trim for front doors
Floor carpets <u>not</u> required
Bronze velvet seats as basic
Under bonnet lamps <u>not</u> required
Manual steering fitted
Heavy duty rear springs fitted
Leathercloth tool cover and leathercloth spare wheel cover fitted
Head restraints <u>not</u> required
Wheelarch carpets <u>not</u> required

Later Police Range Rovers

As the Range Rover's levels of luxury increased, Police
Specification became a determined effort to reduce costs as much
as possible by deleting any equipment that was considered to be
a luxury. Initially this meant features like alloy wheels, electric
windows, central locking and any boot trim, but as luxury items
became an integral part of the Range Rover, it became increasingly difficult to remove them without incurring additional cost.

The drive for cost reduction was always present, however, and few if any Police Range Rover Classics were fitted with a front spoiler (although the fog / driving lights were retained) or anything but the most basic of boot trim. Even the very last Police Classics had their alloy wheels replaced by Discovery steel wheels in white, gunmetal grey or black. Despite the attempts to economise, the last Police Range Rover Classics and the subsequent generations of Police Range Rovers were generally well equipped by civilian standards.

Markings

The markings used on Police Range Rovers over the years were often ahead of those used on other Police vehicles, largely because of the dangerous nature of the roles in which they were used. That said, the earliest Police Range Rovers often had no markings at all except for a single blue light and a roof mounted 'Police' sign, but this soon changed as red tape began to be used. The red tape, which went on to be reflective as materials improved, was used in varying widths on the sides of the white Range Rovers and soon prompted the nickname of 'Jam Sandwich'; a nickname which was eventually applied to all marked Police vehicles.

In the mid 1970s, several forces began to display their badges on the doors of their Range Rovers; one of the earliest examples being seen on West Yorkshire's LWR 964K and LWR 965K, which were registered on 2nd August 1971. The force badges certainly highlighted the individual nature of British policing and they were widely used until the 'Battenburg' markings became almost standard in the UK. Colourful and individualistic the badges may have been, it was probably more important that the Range Rovers were readily identifiable as Police vehicles and having 'Police' in large letters on the sides (and front) of the vehicle was a better option. West Mercia improved on the idea in August 1971 when JAB 787K and JAB 788K entered service by having 'Police' in large letters on a bright orange door.

The lack of a national policy for marking Police vehicles inspired a wide variety of markings and there were always forces who were willing to experiment with new materials or marking schemes. The earliest and most unusual scheme (and years ahead of its time) was that used by Lancashire on their first two Range Rovers, FTC 262J and FTC 263J, registered on 10th June 1971. The scheme, which was used on other Lancashire vehicles at the time, consisted of painting almost the whole of the vehicle sides in a bright orange colour and continuing this across the leading edge of the bonnet and up the rear quarter panels to the roof; the lower tailgate was also painted orange. In addition to the dramatic markings, the Range Rovers were also fitted with a large roof mounted 'Police' sign, topped by a single blue light and two searchlights. Another force to lead the way with regard to marking their Range Rovers was Avon & Somerset and WYA 927M, which entered service when the force was formed in April 1974, was probably the first Police Range Rover to have really effective rear markings and lights. The rear registration plate was moved below the bumper and the whole lower tailgate was covered in red tape with 'Police' in large letters on it. WYA 927M was also fitted with two large rear red lights, mounted below the bumper, with another two mounted on the roof.

As traffic speeds increased, policing Britain's motorways became an increasingly dangerous job and there are few forces who have not lost officers, killed whilst working on the motorway, often on the supposedly safe hard shoulder. The markings on the rear of the Range Rovers then became the most important on the vehicle and became highly developed over the years with different reflective materials, chevrons, etc. The markings were reinforced with high intensity rear red lights mounted on the rear of the vehicle, on the roof, fitted in light bars or achieved by re wiring the rear fog lights. Electronic information signs were also fitted to the rear of Police Range Rovers from the earliest days.

In 1994, at the request of the National Motorway Policing Sub-Committee of the Association of Chief Police Officers (ACPO), the Police Scientific Development Branch developed a new 'high conspicuity' livery for Police vehicles. The pattern of blue and yellow squares soon became known as 'Battenburg' and began to appear on Police Range Rovers across the UK; a West Midlands' Range Rover, H710 OVP, was the first vehicle to be marked in the new livery. The ACPO brief was to produce a livery for motorway and main road Police vehicles which would maximise the vehicle's visibility when stationary, both in daylight and in darkness, from a minimum distance of 500 metres; it was also intended to distinctively mark them as Police vehicles. Battenburg was eventually adopted by most, but not all, UK Police forces and at least one that did adopt it soon reverted to their own markings. The Home Office reported that nearly half of the UK's Police forces had adopted Battenburg by 1997 and over three quarters had done so by 2003. In 2004 the Home Office recommended that all UK Police vehicles should adopt Battenburg or 'half Battenburg' markings and the early Police P38 Range Rovers were generally the last Range Rovers to be marked in the individual force markings.

Blue Lights

In common with other Police vehicles of the time, the early Range Rovers were fitted with a single blue light on the roof, sometimes mounted on a box with a 'Police' sign on it which could be illuminated. This basic design remained unchanged for several years although some forces, concerned about the lack of lighting, fitted two blue lights to the roof. In the early 1980s, the US style 'light bars', made by companies such as Woodway and Premier Hazard, began to be used and were almost universal by the mid / late 1980s. The light bars, which were improved through the years, becoming lower in profile with better lights, continued to be fitted to the end of Range Rover Classic production and into the life of the P38 and L322 Range Rovers. One variation was the Vision light bar made by the American Federal Signal company with the blue lights arranged in a V shape, giving 360-degree visibility; these were fitted to some Cheshire, Greater Manchester and Lancashire Classic, P38 and L322 Range Rovers.

From the earliest days the Police realised that, with the Range Rover being higher than most other vehicles on the road, motorists in front of a Police Range Rover would not see the roof lights, especially at close range. This problem was initially solved by fitting a single blue light in the centre of the front grille; these eventually became a pair of alternate flashing blue strobe lights and probably the most effective on the vehicle. Also fitted to almost all Police Range Rovers from the earliest days were front and rear fog lights; an extra cost option on civilian models. The rear fog lights were usually positioned beneath the bumper but when 'fog guard' lamps were incorporated into the rear light clusters from September 1979, the Police accepted them. October 1985 saw the introduction of a front spoiler with integral fog / driving lights but few if any Police Range Rover Classics were fitted with them and until the end of production, 'Police Spec' continued to include the front fog lights fitted below the bumper.

Emergency Lighting

Illuminating the scene of an incident can make saving life (and preventing further casualties) a lot easier and also enable an effective investigation to be undertaken in darkness. It quickly became apparent that the Range Rover could easily carry emergency lighting without having to resort to cumbersome lighting trailers. Roof mounted spot / searchlights are undoubtedly effective and many forces used them from the earliest days of Range Rovers until well into the production life of the P38 Range Rover.

There were, however, several specialised products which were also used by UK forces in large numbers from the earliest days of the Range Rover Classic until the L322 Range Rover was introduced. The dominant product for many years was the Dale Stemlite, manufactured by Zumro BV in the Netherlands but marketed by Dale in the UK. The extending floodlight was housed on the roof of the Range Rover in what was usually referred to by Traffic officers as the 'Dustbin' and raised by switches on the dash board. The Stemlite was fitted to Police Range Rovers from at least 1971 (Durham's NPT 371J was fitted with one) and many of the last Classics were fitted with them some twenty five years later; a real testament to its effectiveness and also to the development which had taken place over those years (the 'Dustbin' was much reduced in size, for example).

Despite the loss of performance caused by the Stemlite's 'Dustbin', it had the major advantage that the system did not protrude into the Range Rover at all, unlike its major rival, the Woodway Hy Light. The Hy Light featured floodlights which were raised on a mast which was either mechanically or pneumatically operated and controlled by a panel of switches on the dash board. Later versions of the Hy Light were incorporated into the light bar but on all models the mast extended from the chassis through the roof, negating the need for a 'Dustbin' but intruding into the vehicle interior. As the last Range Rover Classics entered service, Premier Hazard introduced the Nightscan system which incorporated the best features of the Stemlite and the Hy Light. Neatly housed the in the light bar, the Nightscan (which was also fitted to some P38 and L322 Range Rovers) was controlled by a handheld unit and could be stowed without either intruding into the vehicle or being housed in a roof mounted 'Dustbin'.

Internal Equipment

From the outset, the Range Rover was such an ideal vehicle for Police work that few modifications were needed to house the equipment for the role. Whilst there were minor differences between forces, the basic equipment was the same, especially the radios which had to comply with Home Office regulations. The early Police Range Rovers had the radios fitted either on the dash board or between the seats, on the transmission tunnel. The lockable cubby box on the centre console, introduced in July 1981, became the ideal place to fit Police radios and many forces did so. Police radios, until the advent of the Airwave system in the early 21st century, were Very High Frequency (VHF) units which enabled officers to maintain communications with a central force Control / Operations Room. Several makes of radio were fitted over the years, including the Pye Whitehall W20 and the Marconi RC690, but the set most commonly fitted in Police Range Rovers from the early 1980s was the Burndept BE540. This robust piece of equipment, which was in service for many years, included a VHF / UHF repeater enabling officers to leave the vehicle and maintain communications with Control via a UHF handset.

The early Police Range Rovers were fitted with two tone horns, often mounted high up on the roof box. These were difficult for motorists to hear and were soon mounted in the engine bay where they were much more audible. Also fitted from the earliest days were large grille mounted sirens which were very loud and often drawing so much power that the headlights were dimmed. The two tone horns and sirens were eventually replaced by American style sirens, controlled by switches on the dash board, in the centre console or, from October 1985, in the slot where the civilian radio would have been fitted.

Many Police Range Rovers were used for speed enforcement work and so were fitted with a large calibrated speedometer, usually placed in a housing on the centre of the dash board. Eventually, the standard fit speedometer was calibrated at the time of purchase, negating the need for the large calibrated unit. Other speed enforcement equipment fitted to Police Range Rovers included the VASCAR and SPDM speed recording devices. Some of the last Police Range Rover Classics and several Police P38 and L322 Range Rovers were fitted with the Tracker vehicle location system, used largely for locating stolen vehicles. Range Rovers fitted with Tracker were easily identified by the four roof mounted aerials, grouped in a square, and by the Tracker display unit on the dashboard.

Police Demonstrator Range Rovers

Throughout the production life of the Range Rover, there were always Police demonstrator vehicles, available for forces to borrow from Land Rover for testing. The Police demonstrators tended to be replaced as the Range Rover was developed and often marked development milestones. These were some of the Police Range Rover demonstrators:

<u>Range Rover Classic</u>

NXC 999M: The second known Police demonstrator. Registered 1973 /1974.

SKV 819W: Four door body introduced in July 1981. Registered on 1st June 1981. Purchased by Leicestershire Constabulary.

A820 KRW: Five speed manual gearbox introduced in July 1983. Registered on 10th April 1984. Purchased by the Metropolitan Police.

C425 UKV: Fuel injection introduced in October 1985. Registered on 18th October 1985. Purchased by Cumbria Constabulary.

G294 WAC: 3.9 litre engine introduced in October 1989. Registered on 14th November 1989. Purchased by Essex Police.

L470 YAC: Electronic Air Suspension introduced in October 1992. Registered on 12th May 1994. Purchased by Strathclyde Police.

M584 CVC: 'Soft dash' and R380 manual gearbox introduced in March 1994. Registered on 31st December 1994. Purchased by Strathclyde Police.

<u>P38 Range Rover</u>

M751 CVC: The first Police P38 demonstrator. Registered on 13th October 1994. Purchased by the Metropolitan Police.

L322 Range Rover

BX02 YMU: The first Police L322 demonstrator. Registered on 15th July 2002.

PHOTO 1 – The cover of the first Police Range Rover sales brochure, published in May 1972. Warwickshire's CNX 802J is shown with a K suffix airbrushed onto the photograph (via Paul Wilson)

PHOTO 2 – Lancashire's dramatic marking scheme, shown on PTF 575M which entered service in November 1973 (Colin Chipperfield)

PHOTO 3 – A820 KRW, a typical 1980s Police Range Rover dating from April 1984. The vehicle was an ex-Land Rover demonstrator, bought by the Metropolitan Police (Author's collection)

Police Range Rover Tdi in action

PHOTO 4 – A Land Rover publicity photo of K383 MTU, one of Cheshire's Tdi Classics which entered service in April 1993 (via Paul Wilson)

PHOTO 5 – Greater Manchester's V344 DCB which entered service in February 2000. The markings are unusual as other vehicles in the same batch of 15 were marked in Battenburg (Maurice Kime)

PHOTO 6 – DK03 KPA, one of Cheshire's first L322 Range Rovers, in Battenburg markings (Iain Kitchen)

PHOTO 7 – A rare colour photo, taken in 1971 in Museum Gardens, York, of North Yorkshire's VPY 682J with its Dale Stemlite extended (Norman Woollons)

PHOTO 8 – Derbyshire's F171 LVO (registered on 17th July 1989) showing the Dale Stemlite and the roof bars with two blue lights fitted (Steve Pearson)

PHOTO 9 – The interior of a 1980s Police Range Rover. Clearly visible are the calibrated speedometer in the centre of the dashboard with the switches for the blue lights beneath it. The blue box between the seats is the Pye Westminster / Whitehall VHF / UHF radio and the black box with microphone in front of it is the Whelan siren and public address system. The device on the nearside of the dash is the Cyfas system, used for updating the vehicle's status and location (Steve Woodward collection)

PHOTO 10 – Police demonstrator NXC 999M being thoroughly tested by Devon & Cornwall officers (Alan Mobbs)

PHOTO 11 – The 3.5 Efi (fuel injected) Police demonstrator, C425 UKV, shown in service with Cumbria (Paul O'Connor)

PHOTO 12 – One of the last Classic Demonstrators, L470 YAC, which was fitted with an automatic gearbox and Electronic Air Suspension (Maurice Kime)

PHOTO 13 – M584 CVC, one of the last two Classic Police demonstrators, which was subsequently bought by Strathclyde (Author)

PHOTO 14 – M753 CVC, one of the first P38 Police demonstrators, shown in Battenburg markings (Maurice Kime)

PHOTO 15 – N54 ARW, one of the second batch of P38 Police demonstrators, registered in May / June 1996 and marked in a generic 'pre Battenburg' scheme (via Jim Burns)

PHOTO 16 – The first L322 Police demonstrator, BX02 YMU, registered on 15th July 2002. It is shown when new, marked in generic Police markings (Alan Matthews collection)

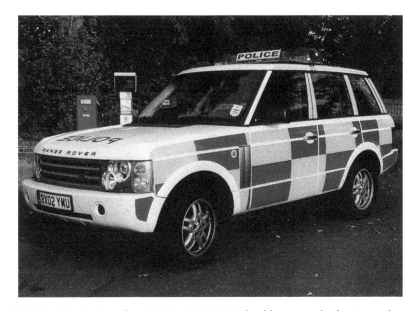

PHOTO 17 – By October 2002, BX02 YMU had been marked in Battenburg and was on trial with Central Scotland (Andrew Fenton)

CHAPTER 4

ROLES

The vast majority of Police Range Rovers were used in the Traffic role, based on Traffic (now usually called 'Roads Policing') Divisions and used to patrol motorways and other major roads. From the outset the Range Rovers were also used as Accident or Incident vehicles where their carrying capability was used to the full as they were loaded with all the signs, cones, etc needed for major incidents on the main road network.

Most forces have had Accident / Collision Investigation Units (AIU / CIUs) for many years. The CIUs are usually based on the Traffic Divisions and are staffed by highly trained officers whose role is to establish, by scientific means, who or what caused an accident. The early CIUs found the Range Rover ideal for carrying their specialist equipment but they were soon superseded by other vehicles, including estate cars and latterly by vehicles like the Ford Galaxy.

Another early role for Police Range Rovers was as an Incident Command / Communications vehicle. The earliest example was probably a Devon & Cornwall vehicle and over the years, several forces tested the concept with varying degrees of success. As technology improved, so the equipment fitted in the vehicles became more complex, but the role remained the same; to establish command and communications at the scene of an incident. In March 1995 Kent became the last force to use Range Rover Classics in the Incident Command role when they purchased four Vogue LSEs from Land Rover and converted them into Incident Command Vehicles (ICVs). Three of the four ICVs were marked whilst the fourth, a 1994 'soft dash' model, was unmarked in

Plymouth Blue. These 'first generation' ICVs were replaced in May / June 1999 by three marked P38 Range Rovers (4.0 litre petrol), which in turn were replaced (in September 2002) by two further marked P38 Range Rovers before the ICV system was discontinued.

Another important role for Police Range Rovers was as Armed Response Vehicles (ARVs). Following the shootings at Hungerford, Berkshire, in August 1987, it was decided that the Police should be able to respond to spontaneous firearms incidents much faster than had previously been the case. ARVs were the direct result of this requirement and first began to appear in the early 1990s. Many forces based their ARVs on their Traffic Divisions where Advanced Drivers and high-performance vehicles were already available. Whilst the majority of ARVs were the standard Traffic patrol cars of the time (Vauxhall Senators, Rover 800s and Volvo T5 estates), several forces had at least one Range Rover as an ARV and at least one of these (Bedfordshire's M63 SBH) was partially armoured for the ARV role.

'Range Rover Weather'

Police spending has always been the subject of scrutiny by the Government (and the public to some degree) and there may well have been the perception that the Police were 'swanning around' in a luxury vehicle like the Range Rover. Whatever perceptions there may be, the truth is that, for many years, there was no alternative to the Range Rover; no other Police patrol vehicle was capable of towing heavy articulated goods vehicles in often appalling weather conditions and no other vehicle could maintain patrols (and therefore save lives) in those same conditions.

PHOTO 1 – A typical early 1970s Traffic Range Rover. This is Kent's GKR 773L and PC Steve Skelton at the scene of an accident on the A28 at Bethersden near Ashford in 1976 (a Czechoslovakian HGV had overturned, spilling its load of Bata shoes across the road). The Range Rover was based at No 4 Area Traffic Office at Ashford (Steve Skelton)

PHOTO 2 – A typical 1990s Traffic Range Rover. This is J190 UDU, an ex-Land Rover demonstrator, in service with Essex and based at the Brentwood Traffic Garage. The vehicle is fitted with a Dale Stemlite and rubber buffers, used for clearing the carriageway (Author)

PHOTO 3 – Greater Manchester's R343 SVM, registered on 31st December 1998. The vehicle is marked in Battenburg and is fitted with a Federal Signal V shaped light bar (Steve Pearson)

PHOTO 4 – The last Traffic Range Rovers were the L322s. BV08 CYC, registered on 1st March 2008, belonged to the Central Motorway Police Group, at that time a joint Staffordshire, West Mercia and West Midlands unit, based at Perry Barr near Birmingham (Steve Pearson)

PHOTO 5 – Three of Lancashire's early Range Rovers at the scene of an accident on the M6 motorway in the 1970s (Author's collection)

PHOTO 6 – The Range Rover's size made it an ideal vehicle for escorting Abnormal Loads and Bedfordshire's CGS 212T, dating from October 1978, is shown escorting a large excavator (Steve Woodward collection)

PHOTO 7 – Police Range Rovers were still escorting 'Abloads' twenty years later; here is Lancashire's L974 HFV (Steve Pearson)

PHOTO 8 – Kent's unmarked Incident Command Vehicle, L820 XHP (callsign India Charlie 1), an ex-Land Rover vehicle bought by the force in 1995 (Author)

PHOTO 9 – Bedfordshire's partially armoured Armed Response Vehicle (ARV) Range Rover, M63 SBH (Author)

PHOTO 10 – 'Range Rover Weather'. PC Obrie and the Northern Constabulary's XST 300V, on patrol in the winter of 1983 / 1984 (S.J. Obrie)

PHOTO 11 – 'Range Rover Weather'. A474 KFJ, one of Devon & Cornwall's last three Classic Range Rovers, dating from December 1983. It is shown at Whitehouse Services on the A30 at Okehampton in Devon, meeting (much colder) colleagues in their Land Rover 109 Station Wagon (Alan Mobbs)

PHOTO 12 – 'Range Rover Weather'. Derbyshire's B67 JRA, a late two door Range Rover dating from February 1985, being used to transport engineers carrying out urgent repairs on a communications mast at Sir William Hill, Grindleford (via Paul Wilson)

PHOTO 13 – 'Range Rover Weather'. Cumbria's E329 YRM, dating from November 1987, being driven by Sgt Andy Davidson in blizzard conditions on the A66 at Banks Gate (a location notorious for its bad weather) in the early 1990s (Paul Whitehead)

PHOTO 14 – 'Range Rover Weather'. Three Greater Manchester Range Rovers (two Classics and a P38) at the scene of a motorway incident in thick fog (Geoff Taylor)

PHOTO 15 – The epitome of 'Range Rover Weather'; a Greater Manchester Range Rover on the M62 motorway near Junction 22. The bridge carries the Pennine Way footpath over the motorway (Greater Manchester Police)

CHAPTER 5

THE FORCES

This part of the book covers the 45 territorial Police forces (often known as the 'Home Office' forces) in the United Kingdom (UK). Not included are the three 'Special Police Forces'; the British Transport Police, the Civil Nuclear Constabulary (formerly the Atomic Energy Authority Constabulary) and the Ministry of Defence Police, or the Port of Tilbury Police (formerly the Port of London Authority Police). The Isle of Man Constabulary, the States of Guernsey Police and the States of Jersey Police are not included as the islands are not part of the UK. On 1st April 2013, the eight Scottish forces were merged to form Police Scotland but the eight forces, all bar one of which used Range Rovers for many years, are included in this part of the book.

As far as can be ascertained, of all of the 'Home Office' forces, only the Dumfries & Galloway Constabulary in Scotland never used Range Rovers. Although the force area covered a large amount of rural countryside, the most important major road was the A74M / A74 which Strathclyde, with a fleet of Range Rovers, policed as far south as Harthope Viaduct near Moffat, effectively negating the need for Dumfries & Galloway to buy any Range Rovers.

Avon & Somerset Constabulary

The Avon & Somerset Constabulary was one of the many forces formed on 1st April 1974 by amalgamating smaller city and county forces. Avon & Somerset was formed from the Bristol City and Somerset & Bath forces and parts of South Gloucestershire. The first Avon & Somerset Range Rover was WYA 927M, dating from April 1974, but it appears that Somerset & Bath had already bought WYA 184M, registered in March 1974, just prior to amalgamation. Avon & Somerset continued to buy Range Rovers until 17th August 1991 when J76 FFB was registered. This vehicle was written off in an accident, however, and so the force's last Range Rover Classics in service were H461 AHT (6th November 1990) based at Taunton and H715 BTC (7th February 1991) based at Weston super Mare. Although the force was never a big user of Range Rovers, Avon & Somerset did buy at least two P38 Range Rovers before eventually buying BMW X5s for the Roads Policing and ARV roles.

The early Avon & Somerset Range Rovers were marked with a wide red stripe on the sides. The force was one of the earliest to effectively mark the rear of a Range Rover; the whole of the lower tailgate was covered in red tape, with 'Police' in large letters on it and the rear of the vehicle was further protected by four high intensity red lights, two on the roof and two beneath the bumper. The front of the first Range Rover was fitted with fog lights and blue lights and the roof featured two searchlights, a single blue light and two air horns. Nearly ten years later, on 10th January 1983, Avon & Somerset registered a four door Range Rover, NAE 803Y, and its markings, emergency lighting and equipment were almost the same as that on WYA 927M, the only real difference being a large force badge on the front doors. The last Avon & Somerset Range Rover Classics were marked with wide yellow side stripes but retained the large force badge on the front doors. The 'Crimestoppers' logo and telephone number were positioned on the rear wings and a standard light bar replaced the beacon, rear reds and searchlights. Avon & Somerset was one of the forces to fit large rubber buffers to the front on their Range Rovers; they made clearing the carriageway a lot easier.

Avon & Somerset's Range Rovers were based on the Traffic Division, policing the M4, M5 and M32 motorways.

First Range Rover: WYA 927M (April 1974)

Last Range Rover: V774 EAE (28th September 1999)

PHOTO 1 – WYA 184M, registered in March 1974 and believed to be one of the last Somerset & Bath Constabulary vehicles (History Heritage via Robert Thomas)

PHOTO 2 – Avon & Somerset's first Range Rover, WYA 927M, showing the very effective rear markings and lighting (P. Biesheuvel)

PHOTO 3 – H461 AHT, one of Avon & Somerset's last Range Rover Classics, showing the later livery adopted by the force. Also visible are the large rubber buffers, fitted to the front of the vehicle (Author)

PHOTO 4 – One of Avon & Somerset's P38 Range Rovers, V756 EAE, dating from September 1999 (Steve Woodward collection)

Bedfordshire Police

The first Bedfordshire Police Range Rovers arrived in 1972 when XMJ 510L, XMJ 511L and XMJ 512L were registered by the then Bedfordshire & Luton Constabulary (Bedfordshire Police was formed on 1st April 1974). From that point on, the force maintained a fleet of about six Range Rovers, the last being A159 UBD, registered on 9th November 1983. When A159 UBD was sold, it was replaced by Land Rover 110 V8s which, although unloved by the officers who drove them, filled the gap until 1st April 1991 when H275 HUR was registered. The line of Range Rovers used by Bedfordshire was then unbroken almost to the end of Classic production, the last two examples, M38 UMJ and M63 SBH, being registered on 1st January 1995. In 1997, it was almost certain that the Range Rover Classics would be replaced by the P38 Range Rover, but it was not to be. The force purchased a number of Vauxhall Montereys in 1998 / 1999 before buying Land Rover Discoverys, Mitsubishi Shoguns and latterly BMW X5s for the Roads Policing and ARV roles.

Bedfordshire's early Range Rovers were typical of the time, with a red stripe on the sides, a single blue light on the roof and a blue light and siren on the front bumper. Although the force markings changed little over the years, the last two Range Rovers were well equipped, being fitted with the 'Tracker' vehicle location system and a VHF / UHF repeater radio.

Bedfordshire's Range Rovers were based on the Traffic Division, policing the M1 motorway, the A1 and other major roads in the county. The Range Rovers were initially designated as Major Incident Vehicles and based at Luton and Kempston, near Bedford. The two units were subsequently amalgamated at Kempston and the Range Rovers were used as Traffic patrol vehicles, with the emphasis being to attend incidents where their towing abilities would be most useful. One of the last Bedfordshire Range Rovers, M63 SBH, was equipped as an ARV and was partially armoured for this role; it was also fitted with a Cleartone VHF /UHF repeater radio, a compact, more modern version of the Burndept set. Since 2014, Bedfordshire has collaborated with Cambridgeshire and Hertfordshire in several important areas of policing and the Roads Policing and Armed Police Units use the same vehicles.

First Range Rover: XMJ 510L (1972)

Last Range Rover: M38 UMJ (1st January 1995)

PHOTO 1 – XMJ 510L, Bedfordshire's first Range Rover, towing the Bedfordshire & Luton Constabulary caravan (Bedfordshire Police)

PHOTO 2 – Bedfordshire's A159 UBD on patrol. The array of blue lights, spot lights and a siren on the roof was typical of Police Range Rovers until proper light bars were produced (Bedfordshire Police)

PHOTO 3 – Bedfordshire's last Range Rover, M38 UMJ, showing the later force markings and the four roof mounted 'Tracker' aerials (Author)

Cambridgeshire Constabulary

Cambridgeshire's first two Range Rovers were registered on 8th October 1975, JVE 524P (callsign Tango 3) and JVE 525P (callsign Tango 33) being based at Peterborough and Cambridge respectively. A further Traffic garage later opened at Huntingdon and from then on, the force maintained a fleet of three Range Rovers until the end of Classic production, the last three examples arriving in September 1995. In March 2005, having decided not to purchase any P38 Range Rovers, Cambridgeshire bought two 4.4 litre petrol L322 Range Rovers, AE05 BLX and AE05 BLZ, and a further five were purchased in October 2005. AE05 BLZ was in service until 2009 and Cambridgeshire went on to use a number of four-wheel drive vehicles, including Ford Explorers and Mitsubishi Shoguns, before settling on BMW X5s for the Roads Policing and ARV roles.

The first Cambridgeshire Range Rovers were equipped with Dale Stemlites and an illuminated 'Police' sign on the radiator grille; the markings consisted of a wide red stripe along the sides. By May 1987 when D113 WEG entered service, the markings had changed to yellow, with a large force badge on the front doors. Stemlites were still fitted but the grille mounted 'Police' sign had been replaced two blue lights. In 1991 the livery changed yet again, reverting to wide red stripes, bordered top and bottom by chequer bands. In June 1990, when G667 WEG entered service, the force changed from Stemlites to the Woodway Hy Light, incorporated into the light bar and this was fitted to all subsequent Cambridgeshire Range Rover Classics. The first two Cambridgeshire L322 Range Rovers were marked in Battenburg over dark blue bodywork and the last five were Battenburg over silver.

Cambridgeshire's Range Rovers were based on the Traffic Division, patrolling the M11 motorway, the A1(M) and other major roads in the county. They were also used for operations involving off road work and towing the force's large incident trailer to major incidents and events. One of the later Classics was used by the force Tactical Firearms Unit as an ARV and for general patrol work, as were two of the L322s. Since 2014, Bedfordshire has collaborated with Cambridgeshire and Hertfordshire in several important areas of policing and the Roads Policing and Armed Police Units use the same vehicles.

First Range Rover: JVE 524P (8th October 1975)

Last Range Rover: AE55 GBY (10th October 2005)

PHOTO 1 – Cambridgeshire's first Range Rover with its Dale Stemlite deployed (Paul Stubbings)

PHOTO 2 – G130 OVA, dating from January 1990, showing the updated Dale Stemlite and the Cambridgeshire markings of late 1980s and early 1990s (Paul Stubbings)

PHOTO 3 – Cambridgeshire's last Range Rover Classic, N899 LEW, registered on 19th September 1995 (Paul Stubbings)

PHOTO 4 – AE05 BLZ, one of Cambridgeshire's first two L322 Range Rovers (Steve Pearson)

PHOTO 5 – AE55 GBV, one of the last Cambridgeshire L322 Range Rovers, marked in Battenburg and cornering at speed (Steve Pearson)

Cheshire Constabulary

Cheshire was the second force to buy the Range Rover with five vehicles, STU 699J to STU 703J, entering service in February 1971. The force then maintained a fleet of Range Rovers almost until the Classic ended production, the last example, L867 SMA, entering service on 19th July 1994. In April 1993, when K381 MTU (and four other Range Rovers in the same batch) entered service, Cheshire became one of the few forces to use the diesel-powered Range Rover Tdi; most either stayed with petrol engines or bought other vehicles. The last Cheshire Classics were also Tdis but the force returned to petrol in April 1996 when the first P38 Range Rovers entered service. At least eight P38s were purchased in 1996 / 1997 and small batches followed until 2001 when Y642 GMA entered service. In July 2003, Cheshire became the third force to buy the L322 Range Rover when DA03 MZW, DA03 MZX and DK03 KPA entered service. The force bought at least one further Range Rover, DK54 HSU, before buying BMW X5s for the Roads Policing and ARV roles.

The first Cheshire Range Rovers were well marked and well equipped for the time. The vehicles had the usual red stripe on the sides and a large 'Police' sign, topped by a single light beacon fitted with blue and red lights, mounted on the roof. Two roof mounted searchlights were fitted, as were two spot lights beneath the front bumper. The rear of the vehicle was fitted with a large 'Accident' sign, a smaller 'Police' sign and a large siren (there was also another siren and 'Police' sign on the front). The Cheshire Range Rovers of the early 1980s were marked with wide yellow stripes and had 'Police' written backwards on a yellow background on the bonnet (making it easier to read in motorist's rearview mirrors). The markings changed again for Cheshire's later Range Rover Classics, consisting of very effective blue and yellow chevrons, bordered top and bottom by chequer bands and 'Cheshire Police' on the rear wing. The radiator grilles were painted yellow and, in common with Greater Manchester and Lancashire Range Rovers, the bonnets of Cheshire's vehicles were painted matt black to reduce glare. Cheshire's first P38 Range Rovers retained the force livery (with the addition of a force badge on the doors and with the bonnet being left white), but by January 2000 when V115 MFM entered service, the force was using Battenburg markings. All of Cheshire's L322 Range Rovers were marked in Battenburg.

Cheshire's Range Rovers were based on the Traffic Division and were more often than not on the county's 214 miles of motorway. With this amount of motorway to cover, and despite having two strategically placed Traffic garages (Knutsford on the M6 and Frodsham on the M56), Cheshire's Range Rovers often left service having travelled very high mileages, even for Police vehicles. One of the first batch, from 1971, was sold having travelled over 300,000 miles.

First Range Rover: STU 699J (1st February 1971)

Last Range Rover: DK54 HSU (5th October 2004)

PHOTO 1 – Cheshire's first Range Rover, STU 699J, appearing on the ITV children's television programme, 'Magpie', in April 1971. The large 'Accident' sign, the smaller 'Police' sign and the large siren are all visible on the rea of the vehicle (BMIHT, Gaydon)

PHOTO 2 – Cheshire Range Rovers from the early 1980s (Colin Chipperfield)

PHOTO 3 – K381 MTU, the first of Cheshire's Range Rover Tdis (Colin Dunford)

PHOTO 4 – Cheshire's last Range Rover Classic, L867 SMA, registered in July 1994 (Steve Woodward collection)

PHOTO 5 – N31 FDM was Cheshire's first P38 Range Rover (Steve Woodward collection)

PHOTO 6 – DK54 HSU, registered in October 2004, was Cheshire's last Range Rover. The vehicle is now preserved at the Dunsfold Collection in Surrey (Iain Kitchen)

City of London Police

The City of London Police, responsible policing the famous 'Square Mile', acquired their first Range Rover in January 1986 when C996 EMU arrived. With a relatively low annual mileage it was over five years later, in May 1991, that H36 YYP arrived and then almost another five years before N501 PHV, the City's third Range Rover (and the third Police P38 Range Rover), was registered on 18th March 1996. When N501 PHV was sold, the City went on to buy Mitsubishi Shoguns and BMW X5s for the Roads Policing and ARV roles.

The markings on City Range Rovers changed little over the years and consisted of a wide yellow stripe, bordered on the bottom by a red chequer band and on the top by a red band. N501 PHV had a force badge on the front doors but that was about the only difference.

The City Range Rovers were based on the Traffic Division based at Wood Street and responsible for policing some of the busiest roads in the country. The Range Rovers also saw some use by the force Accident Investigation Unit. In 1994, during a period of increased terrorist activity, it was decided that the City of London should have its own Bomb Squad. With the Metropolitan Police Bomb Squad based only a few miles away, it made sense for the two forces to collaborate and so the City paid for a Range Rover, M569 LUU, which was based at the Met's Bomb Squad base. The City supplied drivers and the civilian Explosives Officers were shared with the Met. The Range Rover was one of the Met's large M registered batch and was marked in the standard Met livery, the only difference being the City of London badge on the front doors.

First Range Rover: C996 EMU (30th January 1986)

Last Range Rover: N501 PHV (18th March 1996)

PHOTO 1 – C996 EMU, the City of London's first Range Rover, photographed outside St Paul's Cathedral (Paul O'Connor)

PHOTO 2 – The City's second Range Rover, H36 YYP, registered in May 1991 (Steve Mountford)

PHOTO 3 – N501 PHV, the last City Range Rover and the third Police P38 Range Rover (Steve Mountford)

PHOTO 4 – M569 LUU, the Range Rover paid for by the City of London and used by the force Bomb Squad (Chris Taylor)

Cleveland Police

The then Cleveland Constabulary purchased two Range Rovers within two months over each other in 1977. In common with several other forces at the time, Cleveland's first Range Rovers were used by the Accident Investigation Unit. SAJ 41R, purchased in April 1977, was allocated the callsign Bravo 750 and was based north of the River Tees and SPY 453R, purchased in June 1977, was allocated the callsign Bravo 751 and was based south of the river. When the first Range Rovers were sold, they were replaced by at least two Land Rover 109" hard tops; FVN 300V was one, fitted with a Dale Stemlite and designated as an Accident Unit and RHN 613X was another, one of the rare Stage 1 V8 Land Rovers. Cleveland was one of the forces to try the Isuzu Trooper before buying at least four P38 Range Rovers in 1996 / 1997; P870 DVN was the first, registered on 9th September 1996. Further purchases followed and the last Cleveland Range Rover appears to have been X532 AAJ, registered on 1st November 2000 and used as an

ARV. Although Cleveland bought a number of Land Rover Discoverys, they eventually settled on BMW X5s in the Roads Policing and ARV roles.

Cleveland's first Range Rovers were marked with wide red stripes with a chequer band in the centre and a force badge on the doors. The vehicles were fitted with Dale Stemlites, two roof mounted searchlights and two spotlights fitted to the front bumper. Force markings were last used on Cleveland's first P38 Range Rovers; they consisted of a broad yellow stripe bordered on the bottom by a reflective blue chequer band. The word 'Police' was on the front doors and the force badge was moved to the rear wing. From then on, the Range Rovers were marked in the Battenburg scheme.

First Range Rover: SAJ 41R (15th April 1977)

Last Range Rover: X532 AAJ (1st November 2000)

PHOTO 1 – SAJ 41R, Cleveland's first Range Rover, shown with PC David Hutson (David Hutson)

PHOTO 2 – Cleveland's second P38 Range Rover, P876 DVN, registered on 23rd October 1996 (Steve Woodward collection)

Cumbria Constabulary

The Cumbria Constabulary probably purchased their first Range Rover in October 1973 and, with a large part of the county prone to severe weather conditions in the winter, the force maintained a fleet of Range Rovers almost until the end of Classic production. Cumbria was an interesting force in that they used some unusual Range Rover variants, buying at least two batches of Range Rover vans and being the only force to use the Italian VM diesel powered Range Rover Turbo D. The vans, despite the reduced visibility, were always useful for carrying large amounts of emergency equipment, but the Turbo D was very underpowered for Police use (although Cumbria bought at least two batches with the last example, H715 VHH, entering service in January 1991). In 1986 Cumbria became among the earliest forces to use the fuel injected Range Rover when C425 UKV, one of the Land Rover demonstration fleet, was purchased by (or perhaps loaned to) the force. The vehicle, which had Cumbria markings and the force badge on it, was featured in a number of Land Rover publicity photographs taken in the Lake District and on patrol on a rainy M6 motorway near Shap. Having returned to 3.9 litre petrol models for their last Range Rovers, Cumbria decided to buy the Jeep Cherokee 4.0 litre before eventually buying BMW X5s for the Roads Policing and ARV roles. The force did, however, continue their tradition of 'breaking the mould' as they used a number of Volvo XC90s as ARVs.

The first recorded Cumbria Range Rover was marked with a narrow red stripe and 'Police' in large letters on a blue background on the doors. The vehicle was fitted with a roof mounted 'Police' sign and single blue light and two roof mounted searchlights; a large silver siren was fitted to the front bumper. MHH 625W entered service in February 1981 and the markings were very similar to the early Range Rover, the only major differences being a wide blue chequer band under the red stripe and a Dale Stemlite in place of the 'Police' sign and blue light. The last vehicles were marked in much the same way as the early models but with a wide red band and the chequer band beneath it and with the 'Police' sign on the doors being replaced by a large force badge. Some of the last vehicles were also fitted with a Woodway Hy Light in place of the Stemlite.

Cumbria's Range Rovers were based on the Traffic (latterly Mobile Support) Division, patrolling the M6 motorway and other major roads. The Cumbria force area covers much of the Pennine Hills and the Range Rovers were sensibly based where weather conditions were at their worst in the winter; Alston (England's highest market town) and Stainmore on the A66 between Cumbria and Durham. Two of the last Range Rovers were used as ARVs, crewed by officers from the Mobile Support Group. The vehicles were equipped to the same standard as the Traffic Range Rovers, with the addition of a safe to house the weapons.

First Range Rover: (probable) RJM 555M (1st October 1973)

Last Range Rover: M964 PRM (21st December 1994)

PHOTO 1 – RJM 555M, almost certainly Cumbria's first Range Rover, on patrol in snowy conditions (Alan Matthews collection)

PHOTO 2 – Cumbria's MHH 625W, dating from February 1981, showing the early Cumbria markings (Andy Hunton)

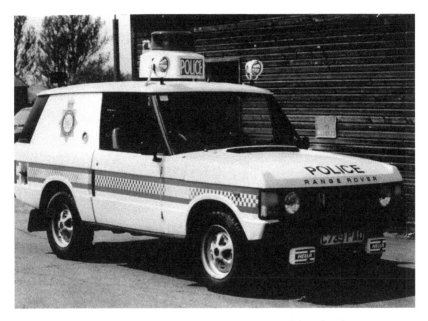

PHOTO 3 – C679 PAO, one of Cumbria's second batch of Range Rover vans, dating from April 1986 (Andy Hunton)

PHOTO 4 – Cumbria's last Range Rover, M964 PRM, showing the later force markings (Andy Hunton)

Derbyshire Constabulary

The first Range Rovers purchased by the then Derby County & Borough Constabulary arrived in 1972; the first was probably VRA 500K, registered in July of that year. The force continued to buy Range Rovers until May 1990 when G715 RTV was purchased. By the time this vehicle had been sold, the Range Rovers had been replaced by Discovery Tdis, K915 HAL being one of the first, registered on 10th May 1993. Derbyshire was one of the early forces to use the Toyota Land Cruiser Colorado with two 3.4 litre V6 petrol models, T949 DNN and T950 DNN, entering service in April 1999. With a large Toyota factory at Burnaston in Derbyshire it was, perhaps, no surprise that further purchases of Land Cruisers followed until at least 2016, but Derbyshire also purchased BMW X5s for Roads Policing and ARV use.

Derbyshire's early Range Rovers were marked with a narrow red stripe and 'Police' in large letters on the sides. The vehicles were equipped with a Dale Stemlite and two driving lights below the front bumper. The later vehicles were still marked with the narrow red stripe (yellow for the motorway vehicles) but the word 'Police' was moved to the rear wings and replaced on the front doors by a large force badge; the vehicle's callsign also featured on the bonnet, rear doors and tailgate. Many of Derbyshire's Range Rovers were fitted with Dale Stemlites and F171 LVO was also fitted with a roof bar with two large blue lights mounted on it; an unusual feature as most forces had changed to light bars by then.

Derbyshire's Range Rovers were based on the Traffic Division and they saw extensive use in the county's rural areas which were often badly affected by snow in the winter. One of Derbyshire's Range Rovers, E199 YTV, was an interesting vehicle and also one of the last Range Rover Classics in Police service. Entering service in January 1988, E199 YTV was originally dedicated as a Headquarters communications vehicle. For this role, the rear seat was (literally) cut in half and the load space was filled with radio equipment; an extending Clark radio mast was also fitted in the centre of the vehicle. E199 YTV, which was unmarked, was always kept at Derbyshire's Headquarters workshops and led an easy life, being used at major events such as the Chatsworth Country Fair and other incidents such as murders. In 2000, with very low mileage, E199 YTV was fitted with a light bar and marked and then issued to Traffic as a spare Traffic vehicle, but still with a control and communications role. This remarkable vehicle was finally sold in 2003, one of the last (if not the last) Range Rover Classics in Police service.

First Range Rover: VRA 500K (11th July 1972)

Last Range Rover: G715 RTV (May 1990)

PHOTO 1 – VRA 500K, Derbyshire's first Range Rover, with its equipment laid out and Stemlite extended (Derbyshire Police Museum)

PHOTO 2 – Derbyshire's E199 YTV in use as a Control Vehicle at the scene of an incident. The yellow extending Clark mast can be seen in front of the roof light bar (via Paul Wilson)

PHOTO 3 – F170 LVO, one of Derbyshire's last Range Rovers, showing its callsign (Romeo Charlie 8) on the bonnet and rear wing (Colin Chipperfield)

Devon & Cornwall Constabulary

The first Devon & Cornwall Range Rovers were a batch of four (ROD 330N to ROD 333N) which were registered in September 1974 and entered service in early October of that year. Another four vehicles, LTA 396P to LTA 399P, were purchased in November the following year and the force then continued to buy Range Rovers, usually in small batches and every two years, until late 1983 / early 1984 when the last batch of three, A473 KFJ to A475 KFJ, arrived. The last Range Rovers were probably disposed of in around 1987 and Devon & Cornwall then used Land Rover 110s and Discoverys; K719 XFJ and K720 XFJ were the first Discoverys, entering service in June and December 1993 respectively. In January 1997, the force became one of the early users of the P38 Range Rover when four vehicles, P591 AOD to P594 AOD, arrived (although P594 AOD was not registered until 10th June). Another batch of seven P38s (R456 SDV, R457 SDV and R459 SDV to R463 SDV) was purchased and they were registered from December 1997 to April 1998. Devon & Cornwall bought at least one further Discovery in 2001 and then bought at least three 4.4 litre petrol L322 Range Rovers in 2004 / 2005, before buying BMW X5s for the Roads Policing and ARV roles.

Devon & Cornwall's first Range Rovers were marked with a narrow red stripe, bordered in blue, and 'Police' in large letters on the doors, also bordered in blue. The vehicles were fitted with a single blue light and two roof mounted searchlights. The last batch of Classics (two door models) were still marked with a narrow red stripe but 'Police' was moved onto the stripe, on the doors, and a force badge was also added to the stripe, just behind the doors. The vehicles were fitted with two blue lights on the radiator grille and two roof mounted blue lights on a roof bar. The early P38 Range Rovers were effectively marked with a wide yellow stripe, bordered top and bottom by blue reflective chequer bands. 'Police' was on the yellow stripe, in large letters across both doors, 'Devon & Cornwall' was on the front doors above the blue chequer band and the force badge was on the rear wing.

Devon & Cornwall's L322 Range Rovers were marked in Battenburg, with the force badge on the rear side windows.

Devon & Cornwall's Range Rovers were based on the Traffic Division, patrolling the M5 motorway, the A30 and other major roads, many of which are major holiday routes.

First Range Rover: ROD 330N (27th September 1974)

Last Range Rover: WA05 OFS (12th July 2005)

PHOTO 1 – ROD 332N, one of the first Devon & Cornwall Range Rovers, registered on 27th September 1974 (Alan Matthews collection)

PHOTO 2 – Devon & Cornwall's LTA 397P, dating from November 1975, seen doing some public relations / recruiting work (Devon & Cornwall Constabulary)

PHOTO 3 – One of Devon & Cornwall's last batch of Classic Range Rovers, A473 KFJ, registered on 8th February 1984 (Alan Matthews collection)

PHOTO 4 – P592 AOD, the second of Devon & Cornwall's first four P38 Range Rovers, registered on 1st January 1997 (Steve Woodward collection)

PHOTO 5 – WA54 DVM, the second Devon & Cornwall L322 Range Rover, registered on 13th October 2004 (via Jim Burns)

Dorset Police

Little is known of the early Dorset Police Range Rovers although one of the first appears to have been WEL 169S, registered on 3rd March 1978. With no motorways in the county, Dorset found that they had little use for the Range Rover but further purchases did follow and the force appears to have had at least one Range Rover 'on the books' until the early 1990s. Examples of Dorset Range Rovers included A483 GJT (1st August 1983), C665 BEL (1985 / 1986) and the last recorded vehicle, F844 WJT (1st May 1989). The last Range Rover was disposed of in around 1993 and replaced with a Rover 827 saloon car. Since that time, Dorset's Traffic and ARV vehicles have included Discoverys and BMW X5s.

Dorset's Range Rovers were well equipped, being fitted with Dale Stemlites from the earliest days. The early Range Rovers were marked with a wide red stripe with a large force badge on the doors and a red radiator grille. C665 BEL was also fitted with a rear roof spoiler which housed a 'Police' sign and high intensity red lights. The force badge was still on the front doors but the sides of the vehicle had been enhanced with reflective chequer bands along the lower edges.

Dorset's Range Rovers were based on the Traffic Division with the emphasis on patrolling the major roads around Hurn (Bournemouth) Airport. The vehicle, with its off-road capability, was considered ideal as a Police command vehicle should there be an incident involving an aircraft. Later Dorset Range Rovers were also used as Forward Command Posts or Rendezvous Vehicles at major incidents.

First Range Rover: (probable) WEL 169S (3rd March 1978)

Last Range Rover: F844 WJT (1st May 1989)

PHOTO 1 – WEL 169S, the earliest known Dorset Range Rover, seen on patrol in Bournemouth (Steve Greenaway)

PHOTO 2 – PC Heath and C665 BEL on patrol near Bournemouth Airport (D. Heath)

Durham Constabulary

The Durham Constabulary operated three Range Rovers in the early 1970s and they were the among the earliest forces to use them. The first Durham Range Rover, NPT 371J, arrived in June 1971 followed by MGH 430L in June 1973 and KGR 723N in June 1975. When KGR 723N was sold in about 1978, it was replaced by a Ford Transit van and the force did not use Range Rovers again until May 1996 when N121 WGR, a 4.0 litre petrol P38, arrived. Durham bought at least three further P38 Range Rovers; P628 WNL in February 1997 and R454 JTN and R455 JTN in March and February 1998 respectively. Durham's Range Rovers were followed by at least one Isuzu Trooper and several purchases of Mercedes ML320s and diesel ML270s before the force bought BMW X5s for the Roads Policing and ARV roles.

Durham's first Range Rover, NPT 371J, was fitted with a Dale Stemlite but was initially unmarked. By 1975 it had acquired a red stripe and 'Police' in large letters on the doors. The Durham P38s were marked in the force's distinctive markings of two yellow stripes with 'Durham Constabulary' on the top one and the force badge on the rear wing. The first P38, N121 WGR, was fitted with a Woodway Hy Light towards the rear of the vehicle and a V shaped Federal Signal light bar on the front of the roof whilst R455 JTN was fitted with a Hy Light on the rear and a small Premier Hazard Minimax light on the front.

Durham's Range Rovers were based on the Traffic Division and were initially used by the Serious Incident Squad, attending all types of major incidents in addition to traffic accidents. In April 1974 Durham started an Accident Investigation Unit (AIU) and the Range Rovers were ideal for carrying the AIU specialist equipment. Consequently, NPT 371J and KGR 723N were both used by the AIU, although KGR 723N was subsequently used to patrol the A66 Trans Pennine road which was prone to severe weather conditions. MGH 430L was actually loaned to Durham by the Home Office and was used by the force Technical Support Unit, along with a Triumph 2000 estate car and a Ford Transit van, to transport the Unit's equipment. Durham's second P38 Range Rover, P628 WNL, was unusual in that it was at least partially armoured. Following its service with Durham, vehicle was sold to Strathclyde Police.

First Range Rover: NPT 371J (June 1971)

Last Range Rover: R454 JTN (30th March 1998)

PHOTO 1 – Durham's first Range Rover, NPT 371J, photographed when it was new at Force Headquarters, Aykley Heads, Durham (via Keith Knight)

PHOTO 2 – R455 JTN, one of Durham's last two P38 Range Rovers, showing the Woodway Hy Light and Durham's distinctive force markings (Steve Woodward collection)

Dyfed-Powys Police

Dyfed-Powys was unique among UK forces in that they only used one Range Rover; J121 KRL, a 3.9 litre Classic model, painted in the metallic Trocadero Red. Although several forces used Range Rovers as ARVs, most were marked vehicles, almost identical to their Traffic counterparts (many in the early days of ARVs were Traffic vehicles). Dyfed-Powys ARVs, called Armed Crime Vehicles (ACVs), were, however, unmarked and J121 KRL was no exception. The vehicle was partially armoured for the ACV role; it was also fitted with a safe for the weapons and a sophisticated communications system (probably the Cougar system, developed by Racal in the late 1980s for Special Forces and covert Police use). The only really visible modification was the addition of discreet blue lights, concealed behind the radiator grille. Despite being very popular with the officers that used it, J121 KRL was sold on 8th July 1996 and not replaced.

First / Last Range Rover: J121 KRL (January 1992)

Essex Police

Essex Police was, until 1st April 1974, known as the Essex & Southend on Sea Joint Constabulary and it is known that PXC 575J, the first Police Range Rover demonstrator, was loaned to the Essex & Southend Joint force. With no motorways in the county, no sales resulted from the loan, but by 1973 / 1974 construction of the M11 from South Woodford in London to Girton in Cambridgeshire was well under way. One of the Essex Traffic garages was at Harlow, almost next to the M11, and it was quickly realised that the garage would need a four-wheel drive vehicle when the motorway opened. Having bought a 109" Land Rover, PHK 518M, in March 1974, the force also bought their first Range Rover, GVX 145N, in January 1975. GVX 145N was a great success at Harlow and it was decided that the other Essex Traffic garages would each have a pair of Range Rovers, a policy that lasted almost until the last Classics were sold over twenty years later. On 1st March 1996, Essex became the second force to use the P38 Range Rover when N703 BAR was registered. N703 BAR was not that popular, however, and no further purchases of Range Rovers followed after it was sold in 2002. In the interim period, the 4.0 litre Jeep Cherokee was being heavily marketed to UK Police forces and Essex bought some N and P registered vehicles for Traffic and ARV use. The Jeeps were less well liked than the Range Rover had been, and the R and S registered Ford Explorers which followed them were even less popular, almost forcing Essex to return to using Land Rover products. The force was one of the earliest to use the five door Discovery Tdi but it was the Series II Discovery which really brought the force back to using Land Rover vehicles. Essex used a succession of Discovery Series IIs, 3s, 4s and 5s before moving over to a largely BMW X5 fleet for the Roads Policing and ARV roles.

The first Essex Range Rover was typical of mid 1970s Range Rovers, being marked with a thin red stripe, the word 'Police' on a blue background on the doors and bonnet and a single blue light and two searchlights on the roof. It was, however, fairly unusual in having a winch fitted, behind the radiator grille. By October 1978, when BTW 35T entered service, Essex were beginning to mark their vehicles in some very effective schemes, consisting of yellow stripes and chequer bands of varying widths.

RAR 530W (registered on 1st December 1980) was probably the first Essex Range Rover to be fitted with a Dale Stemlite, a feature of almost all of their subsequent Classics. When L577 NJN entered service in May 1994, it was initially marked in the Essex markings, with partial light bars as if awaiting the fitting of a Stemlite. It appears, however, that the Stemlite was never fitted and L577 NJN then became one of the earlier vehicles to be marked in Battenburg. N703 BAR, the sole Essex P38 Range Rover, was also marked in Battenburg, with a force badge on the front doors and 'Police' on the rear wings. The vehicle was fitted with a Tecklite (an extending floodlight similar to the Woodway Hy Light) and a Code 3 light bar.

The Essex Range Rovers were based on the Traffic Division, policing the M11 and M25 motorways and several very busy major roads in the county.

First Range Rover: GVX 145N (1st January 1975)

Last Range Rover: N703 BAR (1st March 1996)

PHOTO 1 – Essex Police's first Range Rover, GVX 145N (Mike Lucas)

PHOTO 2 – E205 BWC, which entered service in December 1987, showing the very effective Essex markings, the Dale Stemlite and the rubber buffers fitted to the front of the vehicle (Essex Police Museum)

PHOTO 3 – The last Essex Range Rover Classic, M133 TEV (registered on 1st August 1994), seen in Battenburg markings at the Brentwood Traffic garage (Author)

PHOTO 4 – N703 BAR, the sole Essex P38 Range Rover and the second Police P38 (Alex Watson)

Gloucestershire Constabulary

Although Gloucestershire had used Land Rovers for many years, they were one of the last forces to buy Range Rovers with the first, F982 UAD, entering service on 25th April 1989 (the second, F975 VFH, arrived soon afterwards on 18th July 1989). Gloucestershire's Range Rovers were generally kept for around three years before disposal and so F982 UAD was replaced in February 1992 by J949 OAD and F975 VFH was replaced by K501 TDF in December 1992. J949 OAD was then replaced in May 1995 by a Discovery, whilst K501 TDF was replaced by the force's first P38 Range Rover, P21 VFH, in January / February 1997. Gloucestershire bought three further Range Rovers (4.4 litre petrol L322 models) before buying at least one Mercedes ML320 and then BMW X5s for the Roads Policing and ARV roles.

The markings on Gloucestershire's Range Rover Classics changed little over the years, consisting of a thin red stripe, bordered in blue and a force badge on the front doors. By the time K501 TDF entered service, the badge had shrunk and was encircled by the force logo 'Quality Service with Pride and Care'. The rear of F982 UAD was fitted with brackets on the offside, either for an extending Clark radio / lighting mast or for a 'swing away' spare wheel carrier (it is not clear which) and the registration plate was offset to the nearside to prevent it being obstructed. K501 TDF was fitted with a Woodway Speed Lite, a smaller, more aerodynamic version of the Hy Light. Gloucestershire's markings changed dramatically when the first P38 Range Rover entered service, changing to a wide stripe with diagonal blue and red reflective stripes on it and 'Police' in large red letters on the doors. The vehicle was fitted with a Woodway Hy Light but there was nothing that identified it as a Gloucestershire vehicle. Gloucestershire's L322 Range Rovers were marked in Battenburg with a force badge on the bonnet.

Gloucestershire's Range Rovers were based on to the Traffic Division, patrolling the M5 motorway and other major roads in the county. Gloucestershire also has the Royal Household Protection Group (RHPG) which is responsible for the protection of the royal homes at Highgrove House and Gatcombe Park. The RHPG used a number of Range Rovers but little is known about them.

First Range Rover: F982 UAD (25th April 1989)

Last Range Rover: VX54 JFK (23rd February 2005)

PHOTO 1 – Gloucestershire's first Range Rover, F982 UAD (Robert Stackhouse)

PHOTO 2 – K501 TDF, Gloucestershire's last Range Rover Classic, seen at the Bamfurlong Traffic garage (Author)

PHOTO 3 – P21 VFH, Gloucestershire's first P38 Range Rover, showing the new force markings (Bob Chambers via Brian Homans)

PHOTO 4 – One of Gloucestershire's last Range Rovers, VX54 JDZ, registered on 14th January 2005 (Simon Edwards via Martyn Hillier)

Greater Manchester Police

The Greater Manchester Police (GMP) was formed on 1st April 1974 from the Manchester & Salford Police and parts of Cheshire, Lancashire and West Yorkshire. GMP eventually had the largest Police Range Rover fleet, buying over 270 vehicles between 1975 and 2006, but the force began by inheriting vehicles from the constituent forces. The earliest Range Rovers used by GMP were two ex-Manchester & Salford vehicles, VVM 415L and VVM 420L, dating from late 1972 (VVM 415L was registered on 4th December that year) and PTF 580M, the last of a batch of Lancashire vehicles which had entered service in November 1973. The first Range Rovers purchased by GMP were a batch of twelve, HVM 556N to HVM 567N, registered on 1st April 1975. There were no P or R registered GMP Range Rovers but the force purchased fourteen S registered vehicles between November 1977 and June 1978. From then on, GMP registered about ten new Range Rovers every year until the Classic ceased production; M313 SNA was the last Classic to be registered, on 20th June

1995. On 1st February 1996 the force became the first to use the P38 Range Rover when N461 VVM was registered. A large fleet of P registered vehicles followed later that year and into early 1997 and GMP went on to buy at least sixty P38 Range Rovers, the last being MK02 MBY, registered on 1st July 2002. In 2002 / 2003, having had the largest Police Range Rover fleet for many years, GMP changed to using Mercedes ML320s; a move that was almost universally unpopular with the officers that used them (they were referred to in a derogatory way as 'Panzers'). The ML320s were as unreliable as the Range Rovers had often been but in addition, they simply were not fit for purpose as GMP Traffic vehicles. The force soon returned to Range Rovers, buying at least fourteen L322s with the last two, MX56 AVB and MX56 AVC, being registered on 21st September 2006. Although GMP used a number of Discoverys, the force started buying BMW X5s before the last Range Rovers had been sold. At least six 3.0 litre diesel models entered service in November 2005 & January 2006, followed by at least another five in September 2006. The X5 then became GMP's standard Traffic and ARV four-wheel drive vehicle.

The first GMP Range Rover markings were typical of the time, with a narrow red stripe, a large force badge on the doors, a roof mounted 'Police' sign with a single blue light on top of it, roof mounted searchlights and blue lights fitted to the bumper. The markings remained almost the same for many years, with the notable exception of the bonnets being painted matt black to reduce glare. The first new vehicles with black bonnets were S registered (TJA 257S to TJA 260S, registered in November / December 1977), although at least two vehicles from the first batch (HVM 560N and HVM 566N) had their bonnets painted black during their service. The later GMP Classics were very effectively marked with red stripes, bordered top and bottom by chequer bands, red radiator grilles and the black bonnets. Most of the later Classics were fitted with standard light bars but at least one (K140 VNA, registered on 1st August 1992) was fitted with the V shaped Federal Signal light bar. The first P38 Range Rovers were also fitted with the Federal Signal light bars and the markings were the same as those used on the last Classics. By the time R343 SVM entered service in late 1998, however, the markings had changed to Battenberg with a force badge on the rear side windows and these markings continued to be used when the L322s entered service. The first GMP L322 Range Rovers were marked in Battenburg over white bodywork but the last two, used as ARVs, were marked in Battenburg over silver.

The GMP force area has one of the largest amounts of motorway mileage of any force and includes the M62 Trans Pennine motorway, the highest in England and often affected by severe weather conditions. When the weather was really bad, the only viable patrol vehicles were Range Rovers and they became the mainstay of the GMP Motorway Group. In 1979, officers from the Group featured in a television documentary, 'Motorway', which showed them and their Range Rovers working in blizzard conditions on the M62. GMP Range Rovers were also used as ARVs, by non-motorway Traffic and by the Force Driving School.

First Range Rover: HVM 556N (1st April 1975)

Last Range Rover: MX56 AVC (21st September 2006)

PHOTO 1 – Manchester & Salford Police's VVM 415L on parade (via Karl Dillon)

PHOTO 2 – PTF 580M, an ex-Lancashire Range Rover, transferred to GMP on 1st April 1974 (Steve Woodward collection)

PHOTO 3 – HVM 564N, one of GMP's first batch of Range Rovers, on patrol and assisting a broken-down motorist. In fact, it's a staged photograph and the Ford Granada is also a GMP vehicle (Greater Manchester Police)

PHOTO 4 – A742 HND, the last of a batch of seven two door GMP Range Rovers registered in November 1983. The vehicle is photographed at the Police post at Birch Services on the M62 (Steve Woodward collection)

PHOTO 5 – A798 HND, one of GMP's five Range Rover vans, registered in November 1983 (Greater Manchester Police)

PHOTO 6 – M654 MBA, one of the last batch of GMP Range Rover Classics, registered in June 1995 (Steve Pearson)

PHOTO 7 – GMP's N461 VVM, the first Police P38 Range Rover to enter service, being registered on 1st February 1996 (Steve Pearson)

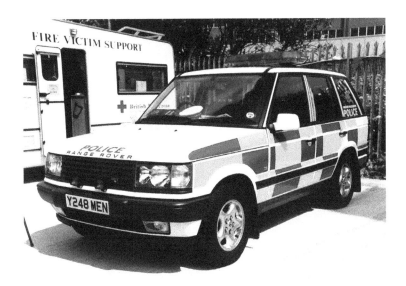

PHOTO 8 – Y248 MEN, one of GMP's last P38 Range Rovers (registered on 1st May 2001), showing the Battenburg markings and the force badge on the rear side window (Steve Woodward collection)

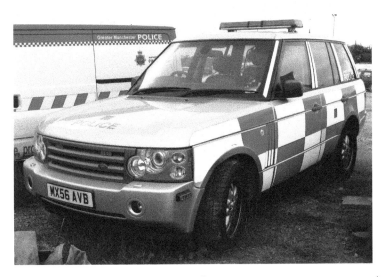

PHOTO 9 – MX56 AVC, one of GMP's last two Range Rovers, registered on 21st September 2006. The photograph shows the vehicle at the GMP Openshaw Workshops in 2011 (Luke Everett)

Gwent Police

Little is known of Gwent's early use of Range Rovers although it is known that the force had PAX 692Y, registered on 1st December 1982, and B377 AAX, registered in February / March 1985. The last Classics used by the force were a batch of three, J288 TNY to J290 TNY, registered on 1st September 1991. There are no records of other Gwent Range Rovers, apart from one P38, T487 KDW, which entered service in June 1999. Gwent went on to buy BMW X5s for the Roads Policing and ARV roles.

Gwent's Y registered Range Rover was marked with a yellow stripe, bordered in red, and a force badge on the front door. The vehicle was fitted with an early light bar and two blue lights and a siren on the radiator grille. The last Gwent Range Rovers were with a red stripe, bordered top and bottom by black and white chequer bands and a force badge on the front doors. The vehicles were fitted with two blue lights on the radiator grille, two high intensity rear red lights at the rear of the roof and a Premier Hazard light bar. T487 KDW was marked in Battenburg with 'Heddlu', the Welsh word for Police, on the rear wings.

Gwent's Range Rovers were based on the Traffic Division and used to patrol the M4 motorway and other major roads in the county.

First Range Rover: not known

Last Range Rover: T487 KDW (9th June 1999)

PHOTO 1 – PAX 692Y, the earliest recorded Gwent Range Rover (via Maurice Kime)

PHOTO 2 – Gwent's J288 TNY, dating from September 1991 (Gwent Police)

PHOTO 3 – T487 KDW, Gwent's last range Rover (Steve Woodward collection)

Hampshire Constabulary

The first Hampshire Range Rovers were GOT 996K and GOT 997K, registered on 22nd June 1972. They were sold in 1976 with GOT 996K having travelled 149,057 miles and GOT 997K with even higher mileage at 178,772 miles. In the interim, Hampshire had bought another three Range Rovers (VCG 667N, VCG 668N and VCG 670N, registered in August 1974) and then continued to buy Range Rover Classics until 8th April 1993 when K539 NTR entered service. The last Classics were replaced by three P38 Range Rovers, S188 NPX to S190 NPX, registered in late 1998 / early 1999. In 2002, Hampshire became to first UK Police force to buy the BMW X5 for Roads Policing and ARV use.

The first Hampshire Range Rovers were marked with a red stripe, bordered in blue, and 'Police' in large blue letters on the doors. The vehicles were fitted with a large illuminated 'Police' sign and what appears to have been an early version of the Woodway Hy Light. Hampshire's last Classic was marked with a red stripe bordered in blue and 'Police' in large light blue letters on the front doors. There was a light blue chequer band beneath the red stripe and the force fleet number was on the bonnet and rear wings. In addition, there was a small force badge on the front doors and the Crimestoppers logo and telephone number on the rear doors. The vehicle was fitted with a Woodway Speed Lite and also an internal roll cage (fitted to all of Hampshire's four-wheel drive vehicles at the time following a serious accident involving a Range Rover). Hampshire's P38 Range Rovers were marked in a very effective scheme of red reflective diagonal stripes bordered in blue with 'Police' in blue letters on the front doors. There was a blue chequer band beneath the side stripes and the side outline of the vehicle was marked with reflective yellow tape. The force fleet number was still positioned on the bonnet and rear wings but the force badge was moved to the side of the bonnet with another badge and the slogan 'Working for Safer Communities' on the top of the bonnet. The vehicles were fitted with Woodway Hy Lights and, sometime after they entered service, rubber buffers on the front.

Hampshire's Range Rovers were based on the Traffic Division, patrolling the M3, M27 and M275 & A3(M) and other major roads in the county.

First Range Rover: GOT 996K (22nd June 1972)

Last Range Rover: S188 NPX (8th January 1999)

PHOTO 1 – Hampshire's GOT 997K, one of the force's first two Range Rovers which entered service on 22nd June 1972 (Author's collection)

PHOTO 2 – Hampshire's last Range Rover Classic, K539 NTR (Steve Woodward collection)

PHOTO 3 – S189 NPX, one of Hampshire's last three Range Rovers, with PC Steve Woodward (Steve Woodward collection)

Hertfordshire Constabulary

Hertfordshire was one of the early forces to use the Range Rover as they had trialled PXC 575J, the first Police demonstrator, in 1970. The first Range Rover purchased by Hertfordshire was WNK 418J, registered in July 1971, and the force continued to Range Rovers until 19th February 1985 when B380 WNK entered service. Hertfordshire then used Land Rover 110 V8s which were in turn replaced by Discovery Tdis (K294 XNM and K295 XNM were two of the first, entering service in November 1992). The force used one further Range Rover, however, which was loaned to them by Land Rover under a special agreement. The vehicle, K429 BAC, was marked in full Hertfordshire livery and was used by the force until it was replaced by a Discovery Tdi in early 1996 and returned to Land Rover. Hertfordshire went on to buy Vauxhall Montereys and Mitsubishi Shoguns before settling on BMW X5s for the Roads Policing and ARV roles.

The first Hertfordshire Range Rover was equipped with a roof mounted 'Police' sign, topped by a single blue light, two roof mounted searchlights and two spotlights and a large siren on the front bumper. The vehicle appears to have been marked with a red stripe, bordered in blue. The last Range Rover, K429 BAC, was marked with a red stripe, bordered by chequer bands, and a large force badge on the front doors. The vehicle was fitted with the Tracker system, indicated by the four aerials arranged in a square on the roof in front of the light bar.

Hertfordshire's Range Rovers were based on the Traffic Division and were initially designated as Traffic Accident Tenders. In later years they became standard motorway patrol vehicles, patrolling the M1, M25, A1(M) and other major roads in the county. Since 2014, Hertfordshire has collaborated with Bedfordshire and Cambridgeshire in several important areas of policing and the Roads Policing and Armed Police Units use the same vehicles.

First Range Rover: WNK 418J (July 1971)

Last Range Rover: K429 BAC (1994)

PHOTO 1 – Hertfordshire's first Range Rover, WNK 418J, dating from July 1971; the force was the tenth to buy Range Rovers (Brian Homans)

PHOTO 2 – K429 BAC. Hertfordshire's last Range Rover, loaned to the force by Land Rover (Brian Homans)

Humberside Police

Humberside Police was formed on 1st April 1974 from the Hull City Police, part of Lincolnshire, part of West Yorkshire and part of York & North East Yorkshire. Humberside's first vehicles were inherited from the constituent forces and the first Range Rover used by the force was VPY 684J, dating from 24th April 1971 and inherited from North Yorkshire. By 1975 Humberside had bought their first Range Rover which appeared, with its equipment displayed and the partially constructed Humber Bridge in the background, in the first force Annual Report. Humberside then continued to buy Range Rovers until May 1992 when the last, J373 HKH, arrived. The Range Rovers were replaced by Discovery Tdis and the force bought Discoverys for a number of years before eventually buying BMW X5s for the Roads Policing and ARV roles.

The early Humberside Range Rovers were marked with a red stripe and a force badge on the doors. The vehicles were fitted with a Dale Stemlite, two roof mounted searchlights and two blue lights and a siren on the front. The last Range Rover retained the Stemlite but was marked with blue reflective chequer bands beneath the red stripes; the force badge was repositioned to the rear wings with 'Police' in blue letters on the front doors.

Humberside's Range Rovers were based on the Traffic Division, patrolling the M18, M62 and M180 motorways and other major roads in the force area. When J373 HKH came to the end of its Traffic life it was still in good condition and so was 'mothballed' at Force Headquarters instead of being sold. When the force purchased a helicopter in 1997, the Range Rover was brought out of retirement and used as a support and ground command facility for airborne operations.

First Range Rover: not known but probably M or N registered

Last Range Rover: J373 HKH (7th May 1992)

PHOTO 1 – VYP 684J, the ex-North Yorkshire Range Rover inherited by Humberside when the force was formed in 1974 (Alan Matthews collection)

PHOTO 2 – NAT 292P, one of two Humberside Range Rovers registered in July 1976, seen on display with its Dale Stemlite extended (Norman Woollons)

PHOTO 3 – Humberside's last Range Rover, J373 HKH (Steve Woodward collection)

Kent Police

Kent Police (called the Kent County Constabulary until 2002) was one of the earliest forces to buy the Range Rover with the first, YKN 631J (which had the force fleet number 1RR), being registered on 17th June 1971. A further eight Range Rovers (fleet numbers 2RR to 9RR) were purchased in late 1972 / early 1973 and from then on Kent's Traffic garages had at least one (but usually two) Range Rovers on their strength. Kent's last Traffic Range Rover was a four door model, C927 SMV (48RR), which was registered on 31st December 1986 and based at No 3 Area Traffic Office at Nackington, near Canterbury. The last two Range Rovers were sold in 1991 having seen service on Traffic, on security duties and at the Chunnel Tunnel construction site at Folkestone. A fleet of eight Discovery Tdis entered service in December 1992; the gap being held in the interim by a few 109" Stage 1 V8 Land Rovers. In March 1995 Kent bought four Range Rover Vogue LSEs and converted them into Incident Command Vehicles (ICVs). The vehicles carried sophisticated equipment for their time; three radio systems, two mobile telephones and a fax and they were also multi role, carrying public order, method of entry and specialist search equipment. L820 XHP (callsign India Charlie 1) was an unmarked 1994 ('soft dash') model in Plymouth Blue, whilst L925 WCD (India Charlie 2), L495 YAC (India Charlie 3) and L776 ORW (India Charlie 4) were all marked 1993 models. The 'first generation' ICVs were replaced in May / June 1999 by three marked 4.0 litre P38 Range Rovers (T712 JKM to T714 JKM) which featured updated equipment such as ruggedised laptop computers and night vision camcorders. In September 2002, these were replaced by two further marked P38 Range Rovers (GK52 NLA and GK52 NLC) before the ICV system was discontinued and the last two Range Rovers were then used as standard Roads Policing patrol vehicles. Having used Discoverys since 1992, Kent continued to buy them for some years before buying BMW X5s for the Roads Policing and ARV roles.

Kent's first Range Rover was unmarked apart from a roof mounted illuminated 'Police' sign, topped by two tone horns and a single blue light; there was also a single blue light mounted on the radiator grille. The second, L registered, batch of Range Rovers were marked with a red stripe and this scheme remained almost unchanged (although a force badge was added to the front doors) until the early 1980s when the stripes were changed to yellow and a light bar replaced the single blue lights. The first generation ICVs were marked in a similar scheme but the later ICVs (the P38s) were marked in a very effective Kent scheme consisting of a yellow stripe with the force badge / logo on the front doors. Beneath the yellow stripe was a reflective silver band with 'Police' in blue letters on it and, above the yellow stripe, blue reflective tape marked the outline of the vehicle.

Kent's Range Rovers (1RR to 48RR) were based on the Traffic Division, patrolling the M2, M20, M25 and M26 motorways and other major roads in the county from garages at Maidstone, Rochester, Canterbury, Ashford and Sevenoaks. The ICVs were initially based on the Force Tactical Team at Canterbury and Maidstone before being moved to the central location at Maidstone.

First Range Rover: YKN 631J (17th June 1971)

Last Range Rover: GK52 NLC (1st September 2002)

PHOTO 1 – Kent's first Range Rover, YKN 631J (1RR), on patrol when it was new (Kent Police)

PHOTO 2 – PC Ken Bishop and HKP 396L (13RR) go off roading in the winter of 1975 (Ken Bishop)

PHOTO 3 – KKG 704P (20RR) taking part in a joint Police / Kent Fire Brigade exercise at Thameside Fire Station, Northfleet, in the late 1970s (via Ron Gamage)

PHOTO 4 – UKO 674X (44RR), dating from December 1981, shown at No 3 Area Traffic Office at Nackington near Canterbury (Steve Woodward collection)

PHOTO 5 – A poor quality image, but the only one known of Kent's last Traffic Range Rover, C927 SMV (48RR) (Steve Woodward collection)

PHOTO 6 – One of the first Kent ICVs, L925 WCD (RRIC2), based on the Force Tactical Team at Nackington (Author)

PHOTO 7 – T712 JKM (RRIC5), registered in April 1999, showing the effective Kent markings which were first used on the new ICVs. The vehicle is shown at Nackington (Author)

PHOTO 8 – GK52 NLA (RRIC9), one of the last two Kent Range Rovers, dating from September 2002. The vehicle's Roads Policing callsign, Tango Delta 42, is visible in the rear side window (Paul Armstrong)

Lancashire Constabulary

Lancashire was one of the early forces to buy Range Rovers with two, FTC 262J and FTC 263J, being registered on 10th June 1971. The force continued to buy Range Rovers until the end of Classic production; N901 FFR was the last Lancashire Classic, being registered on 23rd November 1995. Lancashire then became one of the early forces to buy the P38 Range Rover with three being purchased in April 1996. They were intended to be registered as N196 LFR to N198 LFR but for a number of reasons, only N196 LFR was actually registered as such; it was issued to the force Driving School and subsequently to the Underwater Search Unit. The vehicle intended to be N197 LFR was registered in August 1996 as P982 SHG (although photographs exist of it as N197 LFR) and the vehicle intended to be N198 LFR was registered on 13th January 1997 as P983 SHG. The force bought several more P38 Range Rovers before buying at least eight L332 Range Rovers, the last being PN04 JJL, a 3.0 litre diesel model which entered service in 2004 and was finally sold in 2019. Lancashire bought at least one diesel Mercedes ML270 in 2002 and they also bought some Mitsubishi Shoguns before settling on BMW X5s for the Roads Policing and ARV roles.

Lancashire was a force prepared to experiment with markings and this began with their early (J, K and M registered) Range Rovers which were marked in a very dramatic scheme with almost all of the vehicle being painted bright orange. The only white areas on the vehicles were the roof, the bonnet and a small area on the lower rear wings. The doors featured a large force badge and the vehicles were fitted with a large illuminated 'Police' sign with a single blue light and two roof mounted searchlights. The rear of the vehicle was fitted with a large illuminated sign (as fitted to Cheshire's first Range Rovers) and a smaller sign just below roof level on the upper tailgate. Lancashire's Range Rovers in the early 1980s were white but the doors were still painted in the bright orange. These vehicles were fitted with a Dale Stemlite, a rear roof spoiler with an illuminated 'Police' sign and high intensity red lights and two blue lights on the bonnet (which was partially painted matt black). By March 1986 when C663 GBV (one of the last two door Police Range Rovers) entered service, the equipment was the same but the markings had changed to a narrow red stripe with a thin reflective blue line in the centre of it and 'Police' on the red stripe on the rear wings. The rear of Lancashire's Range Rovers was always well marked and in the late 1980s the markings consisted of red chequer bands on most of the tailgates and rear quarter panels.

The markings on Lancashire's last Classic were largely the same (with the notable exception of red and yellow chevrons on the rear of the vehicle) but the first P38 Range Rovers were marked in a scheme which had been tried on some of the last Classics. It consisted of blue chevrons on a yellow background, bordered on top by blue chequer band. The front doors featured a force badge and 'Police' large letters featured lower down on the doors. The radiator grille and rear quarter panels were painted yellow and the blue chequer band also outlined the roof. Having entered service in the new livery, P983 SHG was subsequently marked in Battenburg but then T199 ECK, which entered service in August 1999, was marked in the same livery as Lancashire's last Classic. The first Lancashire L322 Range Rovers were marked in Battenburg on silver vehicles and the last L322, PN04 JJL, was marked in Battenburg on a white vehicle. At least one of Lancashire's P38 Range Rovers was fitted with the V shaped Federal Signal light bar (as were two of the L322s) but most of the L322s were fitted with a light bar made by RSG Engineering.

Lancashire's Range Rovers were based on the Traffic Division, patrolling the M6, M55, M58, M61, M62, M65 and M66 motorways and other major roads in the county.

First Range Rover: FTC 262J (10th June 1971)

Last Range Rover: PN04 JJL (9th March 2004)

PHOTO 1 – FTC 263J, one of Lancashire's first two Range Rovers, shown displayed with its equipment (via Karl Dillon)

PHOTO 2 – Lancashire's markings in the 1980s, shown on D911 VBV which entered service in February 1987 (Steve Pearson)

PHOTO 3 – The new Lancashire markings shown on M436 TFV which entered service in February 1995 (Steve Woodward collection)

PHOTO 4 – Lancashire' last Classic, N901 FFR, in the force workshops before it entered service (Lancashire Constabulary)

PHOTO 5 – P997 SHG, one of Lancashire's early P38 Range Rovers, registered on 31st December 1997 (Steve Woodward collection)

PHOTO 6 – Lancashire's last Range Rover, PN04 JJL, a 3.0 litre diesel model (Shaun Henderson)

Leicestershire Constabulary

The first Leicestershire Range Rovers were GNR 17N and GNR 18N which entered service in November 1974 and January 1975 respectively. The force continued to buy Range Rovers and in October 1981 they became one of the first to use the four door Range Rover when SKV 819W arrived. The vehicle was purchased from Land Rover Ltd and was almost certainly the first Police four door demonstrator, being part of the fleet for the launch of the four door Range Rover on 7th July 1981. Although the force leased one further Range Rover (F528 URW) in 1989, Leicestershire's last Range Rovers were a batch of three, D21 BUT to D23 BUT, registered in May 1987. When these vehicles were due for replacement, the force bought the first of many Isuzu Troopers (subsequently badged as Vauxhall Montereys) before buying BMW X5s for the Roads Policing and ARV roles.

Leicestershire's first Range Rover was marked with a wide red stripe, 'Police' in large letters on the doors and 'Police' in white letters on a blue background on the bonnet. The vehicle was fitted with a Dale Stemlite and blue lights and a siren on the radiator grille. The markings did not change much over the next twelve years, the only major differences being the addition of a force badge on the rear doors and a Woodway Hy Light in place of the Stemlite.

Leicestershire's Range Rovers were based on the Traffic Division, patrolling the M1, M6, M42 and M69 motorways and other busy roads in the county.

First Range Rover: GNR 17N (November 1974)

Last Range Rover: D23 BUT (May 1987)

PHOTO 1 – Leicestershire's first Range Rover, GNR 17N, and PC Coltman, photographed on a sunny 'early turn' shift on the newly opened M69 motorway (A. Coltman)

PHOTO 2 – D23 BUT, Leicestershire's last Range Rover, on the M69 motorway. The silver pole for the Woodway Hy Light is visible between the officers (Leicestershire Constabulary)

PHOTO 3 — The last Range Rover used by Leicestershire was F528 URW, leased from Land Rover (Chris Taylor)

Lincolnshire Police

The Lincolnshire Constabulary, as it was called at the time, was the first Police force to buy the Range Rover. Two vehicles were ordered, both being built on 21st December 1970 and dispatched from the factory the following day. The two Range Rovers VFW 918J (Chassis number 35500299A) and VFW 919J (Chassis number 35500298A) were supplied by J.R.J. Mansbridge, the Land Rover dealer in Lincoln, and were registered on 29th January 1971. Despite being the first force to buy the Range Rover, with no motorway mileage Lincolnshire found that they had little use for the vehicle and no further purchases were made.

When they entered service, Lincolnshire's Range Rovers were marked with a red stripe and fitted with a small roof mounted 'Police' sign and a single blue light. The force quickly realised that the lighting in particular was inadequate and the vehicles were soon fitted with a much larger roof sign, roof mounted searchlights and driving lights beneath the front bumper; a siren was mounted on the bumper itself.

Lincolnshire's Range Rovers were based on the Traffic Division and generally used as supervisor's vehicles, patrolling the A1 and other major roads in the county.

First / Last Range Rovers: VFW 918J and VFW 919J (29th January 1971)

PHOTO 1 – Lincolnshire's VFW 918J seen with its original markings and equipment escorting an Abnormal Load (Author's collection)

PHOTO 2 – VFW 918J with the larger roof sign, roof mounted searchlights, driving lights and siren, all fitted after the vehicle entered service (Lincolnshire Police)

Merseyside Police

Merseyside Police was formed on 1st April 1974 from the old Liverpool & Bootle Constabulary and parts of Lancashire and Cheshire. It is almost certain that Merseyside's first Range Rover was JLV 761P, registered on 3rd March 1976, and the force continued to buy Range Rovers until November 1995 when the last Classic arrived. Merseyside do not appear to have bought any P38 Range Rovers but they did buy at least three L322 models the last being PN57 USY, a 4.4 litre petrol model, which entered service in December 2007. The force then bought BMW X5s (and at least one Volvo XC90) for the Roads Policing and ARV roles.

The early Merseyside Range Rovers were marked with an orange stripe, apart from the doors which were left white and had a force badge on them. The 'Police' roof sign was more like a neon sign than the usual light box and it was topped by a single blue light. The vehicles were fitted with two roof mounted searchlights and two driving light below the front bumper. Merseyside's T and W registered Range Rovers had the same markings apart from black bonnets, but by the time J65 KBG entered service in August 1991, the force had designed a new marking scheme. The sides of the Range Rover featured a yellow stripe with two thin reflective stripes above it, one blue and one green, and there was a force badge on the front doors. Although Merseyside's L322 Range Rovers were marked in Battenburg, they retained the blue and green stripes and 'Police' along the bottom of the doors.

Merseyside's Range Rovers were based on the Traffic Division, patrolling the M53, M57 and M62 motorways and other major roads in the force area.

First Range Rover (probable): JLV 761P (3rd March 1976)

Last Range Rover: PN57 USY (5th December 2007)

125

PHOTO 1 – JLV 761P, almost certainly Merseyside's first Range Rover (Neild Skidmore via Bob Woosey)

PHOTO 2 – Merseyside's last Range Rover Classic, N753 WRA (Tony Gavin)

PHOTO 3 – PN57 USY, Merseyside's last Range Rover (Mark Price collection)

Metropolitan Police

The Metropolitan Police ('the Met') is the UK's largest Police force in terms of officer numbers and as well as the usual Traffic / Roads Policing role, the force also has a number of specialist and unique roles, including bomb disposal and the protection of the royal family and high-ranking politicians.

The Met's first Range Rovers, a batch of least four (TJJ 380M to TJJ 383M), entered service in August and September 1973 and were probably all issued to the Bomb Squad. The Met continued to buy Range Rovers in large numbers until January 1996 when N760 OYR, their last Classic, arrived. The force then stayed with Range Rovers, buying their first two P38 models (M751 CVC and M752 CVC, both ex-Land Rover demonstrators) in March 1997 and their first recorded L322 model in December 2004. In November 2017 the Met became the only force to use the L405 Range Rover as a marked Police vehicle when four vehicles, all 3.0 litre V6 diesel models, were purchased and issued to the Special Escort Group (SEG). Although still using Range Rovers at the time of writing, the Met have also bought a number of Mitsubishi Shoguns and BMW X5s for the Roads Policing and ARV roles.

The Met's first Range Rovers were simply marked, with a force badge on the doors, a single blue light and two roof mounted searchlights. In addition, two blue lights were fitted on the radiator grille and two sirens were mounted on the front bumper. By the time GUU 104W entered service in September 1980, the markings had changed to a stripe of red / yellow / red in equal widths, with the force badge and 'Police' on the doors. This was the beginning of the Met marking scheme which lasted until the L405 Range Rovers entered service over 27 years later. It was developed over the years as reflective materials improved and the force badge had the Met's logo 'Working for a Safer London' added under it. One exception was K895 FHM, registered on 4th March 1993, which was one of the early Police Range Rovers to be marked in what was then the experimental Battenburg scheme (although the Met was one of several forces that reverted to their own marking schemes). The L405 Range Rovers were all marked in Battenburg on white vehicles with the force badge on the front doors.

The Met's Traffic Division (also known as CO15 and the Traffic Operational Command Unit) had four garages around London: North (TDQ), South, (TDP), East (TDJ) and West (TDV) and a small central garage at Buckingham Palace Road (TDC). There were at least eleven other garages which have closed over the years. The Met's Traffic officers used Range Rovers for many years and the first appears to have been HUV 839N, registered on 11th March 1975. N760 OYR, the Met's last Classic, was a Traffic vehicle and the Division also used some P38 and L322 Range Rovers.

The Met's SEG was originally formed in the 1980s as part of Traffic before joining the Royalty Protection Branch in the 1990s and then becoming part of Royalty & Specialist Protection Command in April 2015. The role of the SEG is to provide armed escorts for members of the royal family, protected members of the government, visiting royalty, heads of state and other visiting dignitaries. It also provides armed vehicle escorts for valuable, hazardous and protected loads and high-risk prisoners. The SEG and their vehicles are a familiar sight on London's streets as they perform their role at high profile events in front of the world's press and millions of tourists. One of the SEG's most high-profile tasks was on 6th September 1997 when their P38 Range Rover, M751 CVC, escorted the coffin of Diana, Princess of Wales on its journey from London to Althorp in Northamptonshire. The SEG has used Range Rovers for many years and continues to do so with the four marked L405 models.

The Met's Bomb Squad (also known as SO13, the Anti-Terrorist Branch and Counter Terrorism Command), was originally formed in January 1971 to counter the threat posed by the 'Angry Brigade', a left-wing terrorist group active in England in the early 1970s. The Bomb Squad soon became a familiar sight on London's streets during periods of terrorist activity and they found the Range Rover ideal for carrying their large amounts of specialised equipment. The Bomb Squad used at least one of the Met's earliest Range Rovers (TJJ 382M, dating from August 1973) and they continued to use Range Rovers until production of the Classic ended. As a general rule, the Bomb Squad's vehicles were in service far longer than other Police vehicles, one example being B708 VYR, their Range Rover van dating from August 1984, which was still in service in 1996, albeit being used for off road driver training. The Bomb Squad was issued with several Range Rovers from the Met's large batch of M registered Classics, purchased in 1994. They were very well equipped with the rear seat being removed to house the 'Cyclops' remote-controlled bomb disposal system and the rear windows being blanked out to make a four door van; the entire rear load space was packed with equipment. The Bomb Squad continued to use Range Rovers, both P38 and L322 models, before going on to use Mercedes Sprinter vans and Discoverys.

Until April 2015 when they were merged to form the Royalty & Specialist Protection Command (RaSP), the Met had two distinct units responsible for armed protection in the capital and both of them used Range Rovers for many years (the Diplomatic Protection Group, responsible for the armed protection of embassies and many other roles, has never used Range Rovers). One was Specialist Protection (SO1) which provided armed personal protection services for ministers and public officials at threat from terrorism and also visiting heads of government and other public figures. The other group was Royalty Protection (SO14), responsible for the protection of the monarch and other members of the royal family.

One of the politicians at the highest risk for many years (and therefore protected by SO1) was The Reverend Doctor Ian Paisley, a loyalist politician and a Protestant religious leader from Northern Ireland who sat in the House of Commons as the Member of Parliament for North Antrim from 1970 until 2010. Dr Paisley was a very tall, stocky man and to protect him, SO1 used one of the most remarkable Range Rovers ever produced. The Range Rover, A161 SYR, began life as a standard Lincoln Green four door model, fitted with a three-speed automatic gearbox. It was purchased by the Met in October 1982 and sent to Spencer Abbott Ltd in Birmingham where it was stretched to 110 inches (a vinyl roof concealed the stretch) and then fully armoured; it weighed over three tons on its return to London. To cope with the additional weight, the vehicle was sent to Janspeed Engineering Ltd at Salisbury, Wiltshire, for engine modifications which included work on the cylinder heads, carburettors and exhaust system (twin fuel tanks were also fitted). This incredible vehicle was finally registered on 1st August 1983 and was still in service in 1996 having covered only 62,000 miles.

In June 1988, US President Reagan visited the UK and part of the preparation for his visit included a number of Range Rovers being issued to SO1. The vehicles, all armoured to varying degrees and fitted with sophisticated support and anti-tamper systems, were easily identified by their thick armoured windscreens, and Land Rover style wheels, painted silver and fitted with run flat tyres. To cope with the additional weight, the vehicles were fitted with US specification 3.9 litre V8 engines (not available in the UK until October 1989) and they were also fitted with uprated brakes (as fitted to Leyland Sherpa vans). These Range Rovers, usually painted either Black (a non-standard colour at that time) or Cambrian Grey, were still in service in the late 1990s. SO1 (and now RaSP) have continued to use Range Rovers, many of them armoured to varying degrees and fitted with sophisticated protection equipment.

The British royal family have used Range Rovers for many years and continue to own a large amount of Land Rover vehicles, including Range Rovers. Often seen in company with the royal family's own Range Rovers were those used by the Met's SO14 (and now RaSP). For many years, the Royalty Protection Branch's Range Rovers were usually green (Lincoln Green and its successors which included Eastnor Green, Ardennes Green and Epsom Green) but they are now in other colours, including Loire Blue, since Aintree Green was discontinued. The SO14 / RaSP vehicles are identical to civilian vehicles apart from the addition of discreet blue lights and specialist communications equipment.

First Range Rover: TJJ 380M (8th August 1973)

Last Range Rover: BX67 EVR (16th November 2017)

PHOTO 1 – TJJ 382M, one of the Met's first batch of Range Rovers (registered on 8th August 1972), shown with PC Steve Dean at the Bomb Squad base, circa 1976 (via Andy Nelson)

PHOTO 2 – The Met's first Traffic Range Rover, HUV 839N (Metropolitan Police)

PHOTO 3 – B708 VYR, the Met Bomb Squad's Range Rover van dating from August 1984, showing an early version of the Met markings (Chris Taylor)

PHOTO 4 – The Met's only Battenburg marked Range Rover Classic, K895 FHM, which entered service in March 1993 (Steve Woodward collection)

PHOTO 5 – N760 OYR, the Met's last Range Rover Classic, registered on 11th January 1996 (Alex Watson)

PHOTO 6 – The Met SEG's P38 Range Rover, M751 CVC, which escorted the coffin of Diana, Princess of Wales, in September 1997 (Chris Pullen)

PHOTO 7 — BU60 BZL, a 3.6 litre V8 diesel L322 Range Rover, which entered service with the Met on 1st September 2010 and was used by the SEG (Shaun Henderson)

PHOTO 8 — BX67 EVM, one of the Met SEG's L405 Range Rovers, shown near Buckingham Palace (Shaun Henderson)

PHOTO 9 – A161 SYR, the 110" Range Rover used by the Met's SO1 to protect the late Rev Ian Paisley, MP (Author)

PHOTO 10 – E151 LUL, registered on 29th March 1988, one of the Range Rovers purchased by the Met ahead of US President Reagan's visit in 1988 (Chris Taylor)

Norfolk Constabulary

The Norfolk Constabulary was, until 1st April 1974, known as the Norfolk Joint Police. Although no records have survived, it is known that the force used Range Rovers, one of the earliest being TNG 450W, registered on 1st June 1981. Norfolk continued to buy Range Rovers, albeit in small numbers, for many years, registering what was probably their last Classic, G713 KCL, on 29th November 1989. As far as can be ascertained, the force bought two further Range Rovers, both 4.0 litre petrol P38 models; N54 ARW (an ex-Land Rover demonstrator) and V261 DVF (registered in December 1999), before going on to buy a variety of vehicles for the Roads Policing and ARV roles.

The early Norfolk Range Rovers were fitted with Dale Stemlites and a red stripe. By the time G713 KCL entered service, the markings had evolved into a red stripe, bordered top and bottom by black chequer bands, with a force badge on the front doors and the logo 'Serving the Community' beneath the badge. The vehicle was also fitted with four searchlights, one at each corner of the roof. N54 ARW, the ex-Land Rover demonstrator bought by Norfolk, retained the Land Rover generic Police markings of a yellow stripe with 'Police' on the front doors, but had a force badge added to the bonnet. Norfolk's last P38 Range Rover, V261 DVF, was marked in Battenburg with the force badge on the rear side windows, 'Police' on the rear wings and 'Making Norfolk Safe' on the lower edges of the doors. There was also a large force badge and 'Police' on the bonnet.

Norfolk's Range Rovers were based on the Traffic Division, patrolling the A11 and other major roads in the county.

First Range Rover: not known

Last Range Rover: V261 DVF (15th December 1999)

PHOTO 1 – TNG 450W, one of Norfolk's early Range Rovers, escorting an Abnormal Load in Norwich in 1982 (Author's collection)

PHOTO 2 – Norfolk's last Range Rover Classic, G713 KCL (Colin Chipperfield)

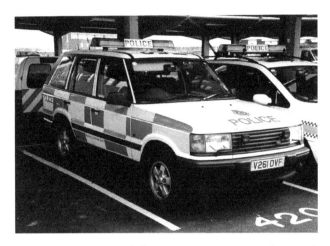

PHOTO 3 – V261 DVF, Norfolk's P38 Range Rover (Steve Woodward collection)

Northamptonshire Police

The then Northampton & County Constabulary was the third force to buy the Range Rover with three (YBD 579J, YNV 271J and YNV 272J) being registered on 4th February 1971, followed by a further three in January 1972. The force then continued to buy Range Rovers until the end of Classic production; the last Classic, M742 ANV, was registered on 1st September 1994. Northamptonshire bought at least two P38 Range Rovers (as well as Vauxhall Montereys, Ford Explorers and Discoverys) and at least two L322 Range Rovers before eventually buying BMX X5s for the Roads Policing and ARV roles.

The early Northamptonshire Range Rovers were marked with a thin red stripe and fitted with an illuminated 'Police' sign and a single blue light on the roof. Fog lights and a large siren were fitted beneath the front bumper and the two-tone horns protruded through the radiator grille. Later additions included a single blue light on the front bumper and a Woodway style extending blue light fitted through the roof in the rear load space. The problem of equipment stowage was neatly solved by Traffic Sergeant John

Mayes, a former coachbuilder, who constructed a 'made to measure' racking system. Northamptonshire's last Classic was marked with a red stripe, bordered top and bottom by black chequer bands and a force badge on the front doors. The vehicle was fitted with Tracker, an automatic gearbox and air conditioning. Northamptonshire's P38 and L322 Range Rovers were marked in Battenburg.

Northamptonshire's Range Rovers were based on the Traffic Division, patrolling the M1 motorway, the A14 and other major roads in the county.

First Range Rover: YBD 579J (4th February 1971)

Last Range Rover: KX06 KYG (2006)

PHOTO 1 – Northamptonshire's first Range Rover, YBD 579J, shown on a British Leyland / Land Rover publicity photograph with 1974 model year vinyl rear quarter panels airbrushed onto the photo (Author's collection)

PHOTO 2 – YBD 579J when it was new, with its equipment laid out (John Mayes)

PHOTO 3 – Northamptonshire's YNV 272J shown acting as Control Vehicle at the scene of a 201-vehicle crash on the M1 motorway in 1974 (John Mayes)

PHOTO 4 – Northamptonshire's last Range Rover Classic, M742 ANV (Author)

PHOTO 5 – Y106 BVV (registered on 23rd May 2001), one of Northamptonshire's P38 Range Rovers, marked in Battenburg with a force badge on the bonnet (Maurice Kime)

PHOTO 6 – One of Northamptonshire's last Range Rovers, KX05 EYP, a 4.4 litre petrol model registered on 5th May 2005 (John Godwin / Emergency Vehicles Online)

Northumbria Police

The then Northumberland Constabulary bought their first Range Rovers in December 1971 when four (BNL 449K to BNL452K) arrived. These were replaced by four more (HTY 37N to HTY 40N) in May 1975 and, although the Range Rover fleet was reduced to two vehicles, the force continued to buy Range Rovers until January 1980 when BCN 898V arrived. When this vehicle was sold in May 1983, Northumbria started to buy 3.0 litre Ford Transit County 4WD vans. Over seven years later the force returned to Range Rovers with two, H347 BRG and H348 BRG, being registered on 16th October 1990. The last in service, H347 BRG, was sold in March 1996 with 138,452 miles recorded and no further Range Rover purchases were made.

Northumbria's early Range Rovers were marked with a thin red stripe and fitted with a single blue light on the roof. The front bumper had two large driving lights fitted beneath it and a large siren on top of it; there were also two-tone horns on the radiator grille. It appears that they were fitted with Dale Stemlites during their service; this was certainly the case with BNL 452K. By the time VBB 82T entered service in October 1978, the Range Rovers had gained a large force badge on the doors and were fitted with two roof mounted searchlights; they still had Dale Stemlites. The last Northumbria Range Rovers were marked with a red stripe bordered in blue, with blue reflective chequer bands beneath it, 'Police' in blue letter letters on the front doors and a force badge on the rear wings.

Northumbria's Range Rovers were based on the Traffic Division with most being based in the more rural parts of the county, on Traffic Sections. In about 1978, the force formed Accident Units, with one unit north of the River Tyne and one south of it. Two Range Rovers were specifically purchased for this role and carried additional equipment when engaged on this work.

First Range Rover: BNL 449K (7th December 1971)

Last Range Rover: H348 BRG (16th October 1990)

PHOTO 1 – Northumberland Constabulary's BNL 450K dating from December 1971, one of four Range Rovers purchased at that time. The vehicle was based at Berwick upon Tweed, the northernmost town in England. The officers are (left) the late George Dobson and (right) Dennis Green (Dennis Green)

PHOTO 2 – H347 BRG, one of Northumbria's last two Range Rovers, registered in October 1990 (Steve Pearson)

North Wales Police

The North Wales Police was formed on 1st April 1974 from the Gwynedd Constabulary and bought their first Range Rovers in April 1980. These were replaced in August / October 1986 by three four door models (D259 UCC, D260 UCC and D984 UEY). D984 UEY was still in service in 1990 and just prior to being sold it was operational during a period of flooding at Kinmel Bay, west of Rhyl. When the last vehicles had been sold, North Wales did not buy any further Range Rovers.

North Wales's early Range Rovers were marked with a red stripe and 'Police' on the doors. The vehicles were fitted with a large single blue light on the roof and a rear roof spoiler which housed high intensity red lights and an illuminated 'Police' sign; there was also a 'Police' sign on the bonnet. The last Range Rovers were marked and equipped in exactly the same way, although they had acquired a force badge on the front doors prior to being sold.

North Wales's Range Rovers were based on the Traffic Division, patrolling the A55 and other major roads in the force area.

First Range Rover: RMA 57V (1st April 1980)

Last Range Rover: D984 UEY (17th October 1986)

PHOTO 1 – RMA 57V, one of North Wales's first Range Rovers, shown at Force Headquarters, Colwyn Bay, when it was new (Peter Coole / Emergency Vehicles Online)

PHOTO 2 – North Wales's D259 UCC (callsign Bravo Tango 50) dating from August 1986 (Peter Coole / Emergency Vehicles Online)

PHOTO 3 – D984 UEY (callsign Delta Tango 50) in flood conditions at Kinmel Bay, Conwy, in February 1990 (Peter Coole / Emergency Vehicles Online)

North Yorkshire Police

The York & North East Yorkshire Police, as it was then known, was the fifth force to buy the Range Rover with VPY682J being registered on 1st April 1971 and VPY683J and VPY 684J on 24th April 1971. The force lost VPY 684J to Humberside when that force was formed on 1st April 1974 (the same day that North Yorkshire Police was formed) but a second batch of three new Range Rovers had entered service the previous September (sadly, two of them were burned out because of wiring faults). The last marked North Yorkshire Range Rovers were a batch of five (LAJ 196W to LAJ 200W), registered on 2nd February 1981. When these were sold, the Range Rovers were replaced by Ford Granada estate cars and North Yorkshire went on to buy Land Rover 110 V8 Station Wagons, Discovery Tdis, Vauxhall Montereys, Toyota Land Cruisers and BMW X5s.

In the late 1990s, following an inspection by Her Majesty's Inspectorate of Constabulary (HMIC), it was recommended that each force had an armoured vehicle of some kind. With the enormous costs involved in buying new vehicles, it was no surprise that several forces bought second hand armoured vehicles from a number of sources. It was at this time that North Yorkshire bought two Cambrian Grey armoured Range Rovers, E415 ANM and E752 KYY, from the Metropolitan Police. The Range Rovers, which had been part of the batch purchased by the Met for US President Reagan's visit in 1988, were based at York.

North Yorkshire's first Range Rovers were marked with a narrow red stripe and 'Police' in large letters on the bonnet; they were also fitted with a Dale Stemlite and an experimental device called an Auto Sensor on the radiator grille. The Auto Sensor was used to detect oncoming traffic and then automatically dim the Range Rover's headlights, but the officers who used it found it quite alarming as the lights suddenly dimmed and the device was not adopted. The last North Yorkshire Range Rovers were marked with a narrow chequer band, bordered in red, and a force badge on the doors. 'Police' was written backwards on the bonnet and the vehicles were fitted with four spot / driving lights, two above the bumper and two beneath it; Stemlites were still fitted to the last vehicles.

North Yorkshire's Range Rovers were based on the Traffic Division, patrolling the A1(M), the A1, the A19 and other major roads in the county. The vehicles were strategically placed in the force area and always deployed on the night shift, usually as the supervisor's vehicle. The Range Rovers were often used for off road incidents and in September 1978 one was sent to the scene of a crash involving an RAF Scottish Aviation Bulldog T1 (a training aircraft) at Bransdale Moor, near Cockayne. The RAF instructor and his Royal Navy student were both killed and the Range Rover was attempting to reach the scene when it became completely stuck in the peat bog. A Workshops Land Rover sent to recover the Range Rover also became stuck and leaving both vehicles in situ was seriously being considered. At the same time, an RAF helicopter arrived to recover the Bulldog and it was suggested that the RAF might like to recover the Police vehicles too. Incredibly, this was done with only slight damage being caused to the Range Rover's roof, and both vehicles were returned to service.

First Range Rover: VPY 682J (1st April 1971)

Last Range Rover: LAJ 200W (2nd February 1981)

PHOTO 1 – YPY 682J, North Yorkshire's first Range Rover, on display at an event held at the Police Staff College, Bramshill, Hampshire. The Auto Sensor device can be seen on the radiator grille (Steve Woodward collection)

PHOTO 2 – LAJ 196W, one of the last North Yorkshire Range Rovers (Andy Hunton)

Nottinghamshire Police

The Nottinghamshire Combined Constabulary, as the force was known until 1st April 1974 (and then Nottinghamshire Constabulary until the early 2000s), purchased their first Range Rovers in September 1971 when HRR 211K to HRR 213K were registered. The force then continued to buy Range Rovers until May 1987 when D48 WVO entered service. The Range Rovers were replaced by Land Rover 110 V8s and Discovery Tdis and more recently by Discovery 4s and BMW X5s.

The first Nottinghamshire Range Rovers were marked with a narrow red stripe and 'Police' in large letters on the doors. The vehicles were fitted with an illuminated 'Police' sign topped by a single blue on the roof and a large siren on the front bumper; there were also two driving lights mounted beneath the bumper. By the time WRC 492S entered service in April 1978, the stripe was the same but there was a force badge on the doors, two searchlights and a Dale Stemlite on the roof and two blue lights and an illuminated 'Police' sign on the bumper. The last Nottinghamshire Range Rover still had the narrow red stripe and the Stemlite but the force badge had been replaced by a coat of arms on the front doors and 'Nottinghamshire Constabulary' in small letters on the rear wings. The Stemlite and searchlights were still fitted to the roof but a modern light bar was fitted to roof bars at the rear of the vehicle.

Nottinghamshire's Range Rovers were based on the Traffic Division, patrolling the M1 motorway, the A1(M) and other major roads in the county. Never very popular in Nottinghamshire, the Range Rovers were often used as Accident Units, held in reserve rather than being on patrol. One Range Rover was 'held in reserve' so much that it became known as 'Justin' – just in case.

First Range Rover: HRR 211K (1st September 1971)

Last Range Rover: D48 WVO (7th May 1987)

PHOTO 1 – HRR 213K, one of Nottinghamshire's first Range Rovers (Adi Faulkner)

PHOTO 2 – Nottinghamshire's WRC 492S, dating from April 1978 (Adi Faulkner)

PHOTO 3 – The rear of D48 WVO, Nottinghamshire's last Range Rover, showing the roof bar with the light bar mounted on it (via Karl Dillon)

South Wales Police

South Wales Police, known until 1ˢᵗ April 1996 as the South Wales Constabulary, bought their first Range Rover in February 1972 and continued to buy them until July 1987 when the last recorded one entered service.

The early South Wales Range Rovers were marked with a red stripe and a force badge on the doors. The vehicles were fitted with a large illuminated 'Police' sign and single blue light and two searchlights on the roof, and two spot / driving lights and a siren on the front bumper. A photograph of WTG 122T, which entered service in November 1978, shows the stripe as being yellow and that the vehicle had been fitted with an unusual triangular illuminated 'Police' sign with a single blue light on top of it; this was very similar to the roof lights used on some early Range Rovers. When PNY 226Y and PNY 227Y entered service in November 1982, the stripe had changed to red but the triangular roof sign remained, mounted on two roof bars. The last South Wales Range Rover was marked with a red stripe and fitted with a conventional light bar, although it had searchlights fitted to each end.

The South Wales Range Rovers were based on the Traffic Division, patrolling the M4 motorway and other major roads in the county, including the A470 which connects north and south Wales

First Range Rover: GTX 614K (14th February 1972)

Last Range Rover: D166 OBO (3rd July 1987)

PHOTO 1 – A rare photograph showing what is almost certainly the first South Wales Range Rover, GTX 614K, at the newly opened Central Traffic garage at Treforest near Pontypridd, in July 1973 (Alan Matthews collection)

PHOTO 2 – A press cutting showing South Wales's STX 172M (registered in April 1974) escorting an abnormal load consisting of the Great Western Railway locomotive 'Dinmore Manor' in 1979 (Alan Matthews collection)

PHOTO 3 – South Wales's WTG 122T, based at the Treforest Traffic garage; WTG 123T was based at Merthyr Tydfil (via David Conquer)

PHOTO 4 – PNY 226Y, dating from November 1982, showing the unusual triangular roof light mounted on two roof bars (Steve Woodward collection)

South Yorkshire Police

The South Yorkshire Police was formed on 1st April 1974 from the Sheffield & Rotherham Constabulary and part of West Yorkshire. The first South Yorkshire Range Rovers were almost certainly LWR 503P and LWR 504P, which entered service in February 1976. The force continued to buy Range Rovers, in small numbers and often in pairs, until February 1996 when N92 CAK and N93 CAK entered service. With production of the Classic ceasing soon afterwards, South Yorkshire seriously considered vehicles other than the Range Rover, buying two Vauxhall Montereys in 1996 as part of the evaluation process. Also bought in October / November 1996 (and possibly part of the same evaluation process) was the force's first P38 Range Rover, P286 JHL. It seems that the Range Rover won the competition because South Yorkshire bought two further P38 Range Rovers, R190 SHL and R192 SHL, in May 1998. The force went on to buy at least four L322 Range Rovers; YN53 HLC was the first, being registered on 2nd September 2003, before buying BMW X5s for the Roads Policing and ARV roles.

The first South Yorkshire Range Rovers were marked with a narrow red stripe and a force badge on the doors. They were fitted with a Dale Stemlite and two high intensity red lights at the rear of the roof. The front of the Range Rover was fitted with two blue lights at bonnet level and fog / driving lights beneath the bumper. The markings and equipment were essentially the same when H442 RKW and H443 RKW entered service in September 1990, although they were fitted with two additional blue lights on the roof and rubber buffers on the front of the vehicle. Having been fitted with Stemlites for many years, South Yorkshire's last two Classics were fitted with the Premier Hazard Nightscan lighting system. The markings were updated with a reflective chequer band along the bottom of the doors, a revised force badge and the logo 'South Yorkshire Police. Justice with Courage' on the rear doors. The P38 Range Rovers were marked in the same way (and fitted with Nightscan) and the L322 Range Rovers were marked in Battenburg (but still fitted with Nightscan and with the force badge and logo on the rear doors).

South Yorkshire's Range Rovers were based on the Traffic Division, patrolling the M1, M18 and M180 motorways, the A1 (M) and other major roads in the force area. They were also used by the Accident Unit, part of the Traffic Division.

First Range Rover: LWR 503P (2nd February 1976)

Last Range Rover: YN55 MYF (2005 / 2006)

PHOTO 1 – LWR 504P, one of South Yorkshire's first two Range Rovers, dating from February 1976 (South Yorkshire Police)

PHOTO 2 – South Yorkshire's OKY 481X, shown having been damaged during the Miner's Strike of 1984 / 1985, despite the addition of makeshift mesh protection (via Karl Dillon)

PHOTO 3 – South Yorkshire's H443 RKW which was registered on 21st September 1990 (Steve Woodward collection)

PHOTO 4 – The penultimate Police Range Rover Classic, South Yorkshire's N92 CAK, registered on 8th February 1996 and shown with the Nightscan extended (South Yorkshire Police)

PHOTO 5 – P286 JHL, the first South Yorkshire P38 Range Rover (Steve Woodward collection)

PHOTO 6 – One of the last South Yorkshire Range Rovers, YN05 OUX, registered on 23rd March 2005 (James Hall)

Staffordshire Police

The first Staffordshire Range Rover was purchased by the then Staffordshire County & Stoke on Trent Constabulary in January 1972. The force reformed as Staffordshire Police on 1st April 1974 and continued to buy Range Rovers until at least July 1983 when EEA 181Y and EEA 182Y entered service. When these were sold, the Range Rovers were replaced by Land Rover 110 V8 Station Wagons and then by V8 Discoverys.

The first Staffordshire Range Rover was marked with a narrow red stripe and 'Police' in large letters on the doors. The vehicle was fitted with a roof mounted illuminated 'Police' sign with two blue lights either side of it. There was also an 'Incident Post' sign which could be placed on top of the 'Police' sign when the vehicle was deployed as a Control Vehicle. When GRF 662V and GRF 663V entered service in Staffordshire in December 1979, the markings were very similar to those on ERF 676K, the only noticeable differences being that a force badge had replaced 'Police' on the doors and the roof sign had been replaced by two large blue lights. The last recorded Staffordshire Range Rover still had the narrow red stripe and force badge but it was fitted with a Dale Stemlite, a roof mounted, forward facing 'Police' sign and a similar rear facing sign.

Staffordshire's Range Rovers were based on the Traffic Division, patrolling the M6 and M54 motorways and other major roads in the county. The force was one of five to join the Midland Links Motorway Police Group when it was formed on 1st April 1971. When the force was reformed as Staffordshire Police on 1st April 1974, some of the force area was lost to the new West Midlands force and so Staffordshire left the group at that point.

First Range Rover: ERF 676K (6th January 1972)

Last Range Rover: EEA 182Y (13th July 1983)

PHOTO 1 – A poor quality image, but the only one known of ERF 676K, Staffordshire's first Range Rover (Staffordshire Police)

PHOTO 2 – GRF 662V, one of two Staffordshire Range Rovers registered on 18th December 1979 (Staffordshire Police)

PHOTO 3 – One of Staffordshire's last two Range Rovers, EEA 181Y (Alan Matthews collection)

Suffolk Constabulary

Suffolk's first two Range Rovers entered service in August 1972 with a third, ADX 920L, being registered on 1st December the same year. The force continued to buy Range Rovers until February 1988 when the last batch of three (E434 HRT, E436 HRT and E438 HRT) entered service. When these were sold, Suffolk was one of several forces to buy Discoverys instead of Range Rovers.

Suffolk's early Range Rovers were marked with a narrow red stripe and 'Police' in large letters on the doors. They were fitted with a large illuminated 'Police' sign topped by a blue light on the roof and there were also two roof mounted searchlights. The last Suffolk Range Rovers were marked with a wide red stripe with 'Police' and a small force badge on the front doors; they were fitted with Premier Hazard lightbars.

Suffolk's Range Rovers were based on the Traffic Division, patrolling the A12, the A14 and other major roads in the county.

First Range Rover: WPV 402L (1st August 1972)

Last Range Rover: E438 HRT (2nd February 1988)

PHOTO 1 – Suffolk's third Range Rover, ADX 920L, with a Bedford RL communications vehicle (Peter Corder)

PHOTO 2 – The same vehicle at an air show in the 1970s (Alan Matthews collection)

PHOTO 3 – E434 HRT, one of Suffolk's last Range Rovers, shown at the scene of an incident (Peter Corder)

Surrey Police

Surrey bought their first Range Rover, LPD 999K, in May 1972 and continued to buy them until 1st August 1995 when N933 RPM, the force's last Classic was registered. Surrey then stayed with the Range Rover and registered P586 FPK, their first P38, on 1st March 1997. Further P38s followed and the force then bought at least one L322 Range Rover, GX06 FUB, a 4.4 litre petrol model. Surrey have since bought a number of different vehicles for the Roads Policing and ARV roles, including Discovery 4s, Audi Q7s and BMW X5s.

The first Surrey Range Rover was marked with a red stripe and fitted with a large illuminated 'Police' sign and single blue on the roof. Also on the roof were two searchlights and a Woodway style extending blue light. Another early (probably L registered) Surrey Range Rover was fitted with a Dale Stemlite but the markings were the same. In April 1994, Surrey was one of several forces to trial the new Battenburg markings, using Range Rover L31 FPE for the trial. The force decided not to adopt Battenburg and their last Classic and the first P38 were marked in the usual force markings of a red stripe with a force badge and 'Surrey Police' on the front doors. A later Surrey P38 Range Rover, R81 NNJ, and the L322, GX06 FUB, were, however, both marked in Battenburg.

Surrey's Range Rovers were based on the Traffic (later Mobile Support) Division, patrolling the M3 (the force newspaper announced LPD 999K's arrival on the M3 at 12.00hrs on 6th July 1972), M23 and M25 motorways and other major roads in the county.

First Range Rover: LPD 999K (May 1972)

Last Range Rover: GX06 FUB (11th April 2000)

PHOTO 1 – A poor quality image, but the only one known of LPD 999K, Surrey's first Range Rover (Surrey Police)

PHOTO 2 – An early (L or M registered) Surrey Range Rover on the M3 motorway in 1974 (Martin Bruton)

PHOTO 3 – Surrey's D685 YPK, a very late two door Range Rover registered on 14th January 1987, on patrol in snowy conditions near Redhill (Lindsay Constable)

PHOTO 4 – Surrey's L31 FPE, registered on 7th April 1994 and used to trial the Battenburg markings. The vehicle is fitted with a Dale Stemlite (Author)

PHOTO 5 – N933 RPM, Surrey's last Range Rover Classic, which entered service in August 1995 (Author)

PHOTO 6 – The first Surrey P38 Range Rover, P586 FPK (Steve Woodward collection)

PHOTO 7 – GX06 FUB, Surrey's L322 Range Rover, seen at the Brooklands Museum in 2011 (Ivan Barefield)

Sussex Police

Sussex Police bought their first Range Rover, RAP 179M, in May 1974, although the vehicle was from the 1973 model year, with no vinyl rear quarter panel. With a limited motorway mileage in the county, Sussex only possessed one Range Rover at a time, each replacing the previous one. RAP 179M was written off in an accident in 1975 and replaced by MAP 885P. This vehicle was in service for three years, being replaced by JCD 206V, registered on 1st July 1980. JCD 206V was also in service for three years and was replaced in March 1983 by Sussex's last Range Rover, WUF 942Y. When this vehicle was due for replacement in August 1986, it was decided to buy Jaguar XJ 4.2s for motorway patrol work.

The first Sussex Range Rover was marked with a thin red stripe and fitted with a Dale Stemlite and two roof mounted searchlights; there were also two spot / driving lights mounted on the front bumper. Unusually, the Stemlite appears to have been mounted behind a large roof mounted illuminated 'Police' sign. MAP 885P was marked in the same way but the roof mounted sign had been replaced by a Stemlite with a single blue light on it. The last Sussex Range Rover, a two door model, was marked with a yellow stripe, bordered in red; it was also fitted with the Stemlite and same auxiliary lighting as MAP 885P had been.

The Sussex Range Rovers were based on the Traffic Division, patrolling the M23 motorway and other major roads in the county.

First Range Rover: RAP 179M (9th May 1974)

Last Range Rover: WUF 942Y (2nd March 1983)

PHOTO 1 – The only known image (from the force newspaper) of the first Sussex Range Rover, RAP 179M (via Brian Seamons)

PHOTO 2 – MAP 885P, the second Sussex Range Rover, on patrol near Junction 10 of the M23 motorway (Alan Matthews collection)

PHOTO 3 – Another view of MAP 885P (Geoff Knight)

PHOTO 4 – WUF 942Y, Sussex's last Range Rover, and PC Wren, on patrol near Gatwick Airport (Neville Wren)

Thames Valley Police

Despite having 196 miles of motorway, it is believed that Thames Valley Police have never used marked Range Rovers, although the force certainly trialled PXC 575J, the first Police Range Rover demonstrator. Thames Valley has always had a significant commitment to armed protection and officers engaged on this work used an unmarked Range Rover, whilst the force firearms team used an unmarked Range Rover van, B313 VJO, registered on 1st December 1984.

In 1991 the Chief Constable of Thames Valley, decided to dispense with the usual Chief Officers' Jaguar type vehicle and instead use a vehicle in which he could work during journeys and also from which he could command incidents if necessary. The result of this thinking, quite radical at the time, was that Thames Valley bought a Plymouth Blue Range Rover Vogue SE, J320 OAC, from Land Rover. The vehicle was then fitted with Police radios, a desk, mobile telephones and a mobile fax (most it was 'cutting edge' technology in 1991). The concept proved to be so successful (in fact, it was the basis of the Kent Incident Command Vehicles) that J320 OAC was replaced in May 1994 by L171 VAC, another ex-Land Rover vehicle; a Vogue LSE, also in Plymouth Blue. L171 VAC was fitted with the equipment from J820 OAC and remained in service until October 1996 when it was replaced by a P38 Range Rover, the details of which have not been ascertained.

First Range Rover (probable): B313 VJO (1st December 1984)

Last Range Rover: P38 Range Rover (no further details known)

PHOTO 1 – B313 VJO, the Range Rover van used by Thames Valley's firearms unit (Geraint Roberts)

PHOTO 2 – J320 OAC, the first of the Range Rovers used by Thames Valley's Chief Constable (Thames Valley Police)

PHOTO 3 – The interior of J320 OAC showing some of the equipment (Thames Valley Police)

Warwickshire Police

The Warwickshire & Coventry Constabulary purchased their first Range Rovers in May 1971 when CNX 802J (registered on 20th) and CUE 391J (registered on 26th) arrived; they cost £2267.35 each. The force, the second smallest territorial Police force in England and Wales (after the City of London), became the Warwickshire Constabulary on 1st April 1974 and Warwickshire Police in 2001. Warwickshire continued to buy Range Rovers until 21st November 1995 when N820 TVC, the last Classic, was registered. The force then became one of the earlier forces to buy the P38 Range Rover with three (N492 XDU to N494 XDU) entering service in April / May 1996. Further purchases of P38s followed and Warwickshire went on to buy at least two L322 Range Rovers; BX06 BHA (a 4.4 litre petrol model) and BX09 VPC (a 3.6 litre V8 diesel model). These last Range Rovers were in service until at least 2014 and 2015 respectively and Warwickshire then went on to buy BMW X5s for the Roads Policing and ARV roles having used them since at least 2007.

The first Warwickshire Range Rovers were marked with red stripes. CNX 802J was equipped with a roof mounted 'Police' sign and single blue light and two roof mounted searchlights, but early photographs of CUE 391J show that, initially at least, it had no roof mounted equipment fitted. Subsequent photos show that it was fitted with the same 'Police' sign and blue light and searchlights as CNX 802J and also a Woodway style extending light mast. Warwickshire's markings remained fairly similar for a number of years, with the same red stripes. By the time XDU 775S and XDU 776S entered service in March / April 1978, a force badge had been added to the doors, a siren and two blue lights were fitted to the radiator grille and the roof was fitted with a large 'Police' sign, two blue lights and two searchlights (with blue lenses). The markings were still the same when DVC 561Y and DVC 562Y entered service in February 1983, although they were fitted with light bars. The later Warwickshire Classics and the first P38s had their sides almost completely covered in red material with 'Police' in white letters' on the front doors and a force badge on the rear doors; they were also fitted with Woodway Hy Lights. The later P38s and the L322s were marked in Battenburg with 'Warwickshire Police' and a force badge on the bonnet.

On 1st April 1971 Warwickshire & Coventry was one of the five forces to join the Midland Links Motorway Police Group when it was formed. When the force was reformed as the Warwickshire Constabulary on 1st April 1974, some of the motorway network was lost to the new West Midlands force and so Warwickshire left the group at that point. Although Warwickshire did not join the Central Motorway Police Group when it was formed in 1990, they did join in 2001, and finally left in 2007. Warwickshire's Range Rovers were based on the Traffic Division, patrolling the M6, M40, M42, M45 and M69 motorways and other major roads in the county.

First Range Rover: CNX 802J (20th May 1971)

Last Range Rover: BX09 VPC (1st July 2009)

PHOTO 1 – Warwickshire's first two Range Rovers, featured in the first Police Range Rover sales brochure, published in May 1972. CUE 391J is shown prior to the roof lighting being fitted and with a K suffix airbrushed onto the photograph (via Paul Wilson)

PHOTO 2 – Warwickshire's XDU 776S, registered on 1st April 1978, showing the force markings of the time (Alan Matthews collection)

PHOTO 3 – Warwickshire's last Classic, N820 TVC, shown at the Greys Mallory Traffic garage, between Junctions 13 and 14 of the M40 motorway (Author)

PHOTO 4 – N492 XDU, the first Warwickshire P38 Range Rover, registered on 12th April 1996. The vehicle was sold in 1999 having covered 192,749 miles (Steve Woodward collection)

PHOTO 5 – Warwickshire's last Range Rover, BX09 VPC. The vehicle was originally an unmarked firearms support vehicle but later in its service it was marked and issued to the force Operational Patrol Unit (Shaun Henderson)

West Mercia Police

The West Mercia Constabulary (which was renamed West Mercia Police in 2009) was formed in 1967 by merging three county forces; Herefordshire, Shropshire and Worcestershire. The first West Mercia Range Rovers were JAB 787K and JAB 788K, registered on 18th August 1971. The force continued to buy Range Rovers, often in pairs or groups of three, until November / December 1995 when the last Classics, N981 AAB and N982 AAB, entered service. When the last Range Rovers were sold, West Mercia went on to buy Vauxhall Montereys, Toyota Land Cruisers and Mercedes MLs before buying BMW X5s for the Roads Policing and ARV roles.

The first West Mercia Range Rovers were marked with an orange door with 'Police' on it. By December 1973 when XWP 724M and XWP 725M entered service, the orange was extended along the sides of the bonnet, the rear wings and on the lower tailgate. The early vehicles were all fitted with a triangular 'Police' roof sign with a single blue light, fog / driving lights and a large siren, mounted on the bumper.

FVJ 22W to FVJ 24W, registered on 1st May 1981, were the first West Mercia Range Rovers to be marked with wide red stripes; a force badge was added to FVJ 23W at some point. Interestingly, although FVJ 22W was fitted with a single blue light, FVJ 23W retained the old triangular roof sign and blue light. In around October 1987 when E838 GUY to E840 GUY entered service, West Mercia started to mark their Range Rovers in a very effective scheme which became known as 'Tiger Stripe'. The scheme consisted of diagonal blue and yellow stripes with 'Police' in large yellow letters on a blue background on the doors and a force badge on the rear wing. West Midlands changed their markings at the same time, the only difference between the two forces being that the stripes slanted in different directions. West Mercia's Range Rovers were marked in Tiger Stripe until the last Classics entered service; these last Range Rovers were also fitted with rubber buffers.

On 1st April 1971 West Mercia was one of the five forces to join the Midland Links Motorway Police Group when it was formed. The force stayed when the Central Motorway Police Group was formed in 1990 and left in 2018. West Mercia's Range Rovers were based on the Traffic Division, patrolling the M5, M6, M42, M50 and M54 motorways and other major roads in the county.

First Range Rover: JAB 787K (18th August 1971)

Last Range Rover: N982 AAB (1st December 1995)

PHOTO 1 – JAB 787K, one of West Mercia's first two Range Rovers, registered on 18th August 1971 (Norman Woollons)

PHOTO 2 – West Mercia's XWP 725M, registered on 1st December 1973, showing the bright orange markings and the early triangular roof sign (Paul O'Connor)

PHOTO 3 – FVJ 23W, one of the first West Mercia Range Rovers to be marked with red reflective stripes. The vehicle is shown at Strensham Services on the M5 motorway (Steve Greenaway)

PHOTO 4 – West Mercia's last Range Rover, N982 AAB, registered on 1st December 1995 (Author)

West Midlands Police

The West Midlands Police was formed on 1st April 1974 from the Birmingham City Police, the West Midlands Constabulary and parts of the Staffordshire County & Stoke on Trent Constabulary, the Warwickshire & Coventry Constabulary and the West Mercia Constabulary. Birmingham City and the old West Midlands force had been part of the Midlands Links Motorway Police Group since its formation in April 1971 and the first Range Rovers used by these forces were a batch of six, XOG 1J to XOG 6J, registered on 26th March 1971. Another batch, which included COA 2K, COA 7K and COA 8K, entered service in January 1972 and the force then continued to buy Range Rovers in fairly large numbers until 1st May 1996 when N973 CUK, the last Police Range Rover Classic in the UK, was registered. Having been involved in the development of the P38 Range Rover, it was almost inevitable that West Midlands would buy them and the first appears to have been P83 JOX, registered on 1st January 1997. The last P38s were probably a batch of four, all registered on 1st September 2002, and West Midlands then bought a number of L322 Range Rovers. The first L322 Range Rovers were 4.4 litre petrol models, registered in November 2004, and the force continued to buy small numbers of them until October 2008 when BX58 MHK, a 3.6 litre V8 diesel model and the last recorded West Midlands Range Rover, entered service. The force then used Discoverys for a number of years before buying BMW X5s for the Roads Policing and ARV roles.

The first West Midlands Range Rovers were marked with a red stripe and fitted with a large roof mounted 'Police' sign and a single blue light. The vehicles were also fitted with two roof mounted searchlights and a Woodway style extending light mast (probably a Clark Mast design). The second batch of vehicles had the same markings but the radiator grilles were painted red and these effective markings continued to be used on West Midlands Range Rovers throughout the 1970s and into the 1980s.

A30 UOC entered service in April 1984 and the markings were the same, with the addition of a force badge on the doors and a light bar on the roof. In about 1987 / 1988, West Midlands (and West Mercia) started to mark their Range Rovers in a very effective scheme which became known as 'Tiger Stripe'. The scheme consisted of diagonal blue and yellow stripes with 'Police' in large yellow letters on a blue background on the doors and a force badge on the vinyl rear quarter panel; the radiator grilles were also painted yellow and the vehicles were fitted with rubber buffers. Effective though the Tiger Stripe markings may have been, it was considered that the traditional red stripe was more visible and so West Midlands became involved in two important ACPO trials of markings. In 1991 / 1992 H710 OVP, a West Midlands Range Rover which had entered service on 11th June 1991, was marked in the first trial markings; a reflective red stripe bordered in chequer band, with a force badge on the front doors and 'Police' on the rear wings. The scheme was not adopted and in 1993 / 1994 H710 OVP became the first Police Range Rover to be marked in Battenburg. Despite having been involved in the two trials, West Midlands did not adopt either scheme and the last Classics and the all but the last P38s, were marked in Tiger Stripe. The West Midlands L322 Range Rovers were all marked in Battenburg with the force badge and the Central Motorway Police Group logo in the rear side window.

The first West Midlands Range Rovers were an important part of the Midland Links Motorway Police Group and the force remained with it when it became the Central Motorway Police Group in 1990. The Central Motorway Police Group is still responsible for policing the M5, the M6, the M6 Toll, the M42, the M54, the A38(M) Aston Expressway and the A500.

For many years, West Midlands operated a policy of 'cascading' ex-Traffic Range Rovers to several other units prior to disposal. This meant that it was possible to see much older vehicles than usual still in service; the force was using E registered (1987 / 1988) Range Rovers in 1996, for example. About six Range Rovers a year were cascaded from Motorway Traffic to units including non-motorway Traffic, Accident Investigation, Birmingham Airport, Firearms, Public Order and the force workshops.

First Range Rover: XOG 1J (26th March 1971)

Last Range Rover: BX58 MHK (1st October 2008)

PHOTO 1 – XOG 1J and another West Midlands Range Rover, photographed the day before the Midland Links Motorway Police Group started patrolling Birmingham's motorways. The officers (from left to right) are: Sgt M. Lloyd, West Midlands Police, PC A. Aitkin, Birmingham City Police and PC R. Allen, West Mercia Constabulary (Birmingham Post & Mail)

PHOTO 2 – A Land Rover publicity photograph of COA 7K, one of the second batch of 'Midland Links' Range Rovers, registered on 26th January 1972 (via James Taylor)

PHOTO 3 – COA 8K, featured in a Birmingham City recruitment advert in 'Soldier' magazine in the early 1970s (Author's collection)

PHOTO 4 – West Midlands' LOJ 392X, registered on 15th September 1981, showing the force markings of the 1970s and 1980s (via Steve Pearson)

PHOTO 5 – H710 OVP, shown in the first ACPO trial markings (Tony Howland)

PHOTO 6 – H710 OVP, the first Police Range Rover to be marked in Battenburg (Author's collection)

PHOTO 7 – N673 CUK, the last Police Range Rover Classic in the UK, showing the very effective 'Tiger Stripe' markings used by West Mercia and West Midlands (Alan Matthews collection)

PHOTO 8 – The first West Midlands P38 Range Rover, P83 JOX, which entered service in January 1997 (via Jim Burns)

PHOTO 9 – BV52 ZLY, the last of West Midlands' P38 Range Rovers, marked in Battenburg (Maurice Kime)

PHOTO 10 – BU54 AEF, one of West Midlands' first L322 Range Rovers, dating from November 2004 (Alan Matthews collection)

PHOTO 11 – The last West Midlands Range Rover, BX58 MHK, registered on 1st October 2008 (Steve Pearson)

West Yorkshire Police

The West Yorkshire Police was formed on 1st April 1974 from part of the West Yorkshire Constabulary, the Bradford City Police and the Leeds City Police. The force was originally known as the West Yorkshire Metropolitan Police and was renamed West Yorkshire Police in 1986. The first Range Rovers bought by the West Yorkshire Constabulary were LWR 964K and LWR 965K, registered on 2nd August 1971, whilst Bradford City Police used KUM 385L and Leeds City Police used KUB 126L (both vehicles dating from October 1972). West Yorkshire continued to buy Range Rovers for many years with the last Classics, M91 VUB and M92 VUB, being registered on 23rd December 1994. The last West Yorkshire Range Rovers suffered from serious reliability problems including engine management and cylinder head issues; one Range Rover was fitted with four engines having travelled less than 120,000 miles. Despite enormous efforts being made by West Yorkshire's experienced workshops staff, the problems were not solved and the force grew increasingly dissatisfied with the Range Rover, going on to buy a number of other vehicles including Vauxhall Montereys, Ford Explorers, Mercedes ML270s and Discoverys. In March 2005, having not bought any P38 Range Rovers, West Yorkshire bought the first of seven L322 models for the Motorway Unit, based at Wakefield. The first vehicles were 4.4 litre petrol models whilst the last two, which entered service in 2008, were 3.6 litre V8 diesel models. When the last Range Rovers were sold, West Yorkshire bought BMW X5s for the Roads Policing and ARV roles.

The first West Yorkshire Constabulary Range Rovers were marked with a narrow red stripe and a force badge (probably the first Police Range Rovers to feature a force badge). They were fitted with a large roof mounted 'Police' sign and a single blue light, with fog lights and a very large siren being fitted beneath the front bumper. Of the first two Range Rovers, only LWR 964K was fitted with a capstan winch, concealed behind the radiator grille. The Bradford City and Leeds City Range Rovers were both fitted with

Dale Stemlites and Bradford City's KUM 385L was also fitted with a capstan winch (the vehicle was still in service in 1974 and was transferred to the new West Yorkshire force). By May 1981, when PNW 490W and PNW 491W entered service, West Yorkshire had changed their markings to a scheme which remained almost unaltered until the last L322 Range Rovers were in service. The scheme consisted of a narrow yellow stripe, bordered in green, with a force badge on the front doors and 'Police' on the rear wings. In common with many, if not all, of West Yorkshire's Range Rovers, the W registered vehicles were fitted with Dale Stemlites and H78 SWX, which entered service in November 1990, wore the same markings, was fitted with a Stemlite and was also was fitted with rubber buffers. At least one of the last Classics (M91 VUB) was fitted with a Woodway Speed Lite which was lower in profile than the Stemlite and with the mast extending through the vehicle to the chassis; it was much more stable when extended in exposed areas on the motorway. The first West Yorkshire L322 Range Rovers were marked in the force markings but at least one, YJ08 OXC, was re-marked in Battenburg during its service (YJ08 OXB appears to have been marked in Battenburg from the outset).

West Yorkshire's Range Rovers were based on the Traffic Division patrolling the M1, the M62, the M606 and the M621 motorways and the A1(M), with the Motorway Unit being based at the Wakefield 41 Industrial Estate in Wakefield. The weather conditions in the winter, particularly on the M62 motorway, made Range Rovers the only viable patrol vehicles for many years.

First Range Rover: LWR 964K (2nd August 1971)

Last Range Rover: YJ08 OXC (1st May 2008)

PHOTO 1 – LWR 964K, West Yorkshire Constabulary's first Range Rover, dating from August 1971. The roller for the capstan winch can be seen on the front bumper (West Yorkshire Police)

PHOTO 2 – Bradford City Police's KUM 385L with its Dale Stemlite in the raised position (Author's collection)

PHOTO 3 – PNW 491W, registered on 6th May 1981, one of the early West Yorkshire Range Rovers to feature the force's unique marking scheme (West Yorkshire Police)

PHOTO 4 – West Yorkshire's H78 SWX, shown just off the M62 motorway at Scammonden. The bridge in the background is the B6114 Saddleworth Road (West Yorkshire Police)

PHOTO 5 – M92 VUB, one of the last two West Yorkshire Range Rover Classics, which entered service in December 1994 (Steve Pearson)

PHOTO 6 – One of West Yorkshire's first L322 Range Rovers, YJ55 YNN, registered on 1st December 2005 (Iain Kitchen)

PHOTO 7 – YJ08 OXB, one of the last West Yorkshire Range Rovers, marked in Battenburg (Alan Matthews collection)

Wiltshire Police

The then Wiltshire Constabulary bought their first Range Rover in December 1972 and continued to buy them until 1st June 1995 when the last three Classics, M851 FHR to M853 FHR, were registered. Wiltshire then continued to buy Range Rovers, with a 4.0 litre petrol P38, P109 AAM, being registered on 1st June 1997 and another P38, WV52 CBU (the last recorded Wiltshire Range Rover) being registered on 15th November 2002. When the last Range Rovers were sold, Wiltshire bought BMW X5s for the Roads Policing and ARV roles.

Wiltshire's first Range Rover was marked with a red stripe with 'Police' above it on the doors. The vehicle was fitted with a roof mounted 'Police' sign with blue / red lights on each end of it and a single blue light on top on it; also on the roof were two searchlights. By May 1986 when C442 MMR entered service, Wiltshire's Range Rovers were marked in a scheme which would last, almost unaltered, for many years. The vehicles were marked with a wide red stripe, bordered in blue, a force badge on the front doors and 'Wiltshire Constabulary' on the rear wings. C442 MMR was fitted with a large blue light and two roof mounted searchlights but these had been replaced by a light bar and a Woodway Hy Lite by the time F964 FMW entered service in May 1988. Wiltshire's last Classics and the first P38 were marked in the same scheme, although the P38 was subsequently re marked in Battenburg. Wiltshire's last Range Rover was marked in Battenburg with a force badge on the front doors and the force logo, 'Keeping Wiltshire Safe', along the bottom of the doors.

Wiltshire's Range Rovers were based on the Traffic Division, patrolling the M4 motorway and other major roads in the county. Other Wiltshire Range Rovers, usually unmarked, were used for armed security duties.

First Range Rover: BMW 70L (8th December 1972)

Last Range Rover: WV52 CBU (15th November 2002)

PHOTO 1 – BMW 70L, Wiltshire's first Range Rover, which was based at the Swindon Traffic Unit (Alan Matthews collection)

PHOTO 2 – H969 MKV, an ex-Land Rover demonstrator bought by Wiltshire and marked in the force scheme (Alan Matthews collection)

PHOTO 3 – One of Wiltshire's last three Range Rover Classics, M852 FHR (Steve Woodward collection)

PHOTO 4 – Wiltshire's first P38 Range Rover, P109 AAM, shown in the force marking scheme; the vehicle was subsequently marked in Battenburg (Steve Woodward collection)

PHOTO 5 – Wiltshire's last Range Rover, WV52 CBU, which entered service in November 2002 (Alan Matthews collection)

Central Scotland Police

The Central Scotland Police was formed on 16th May 1975 from most of the Stirling & Clackmannan Constabulary force area and part of the Perth & Kinross Constabulary force area. On 1st April 2013, Central Scotland was merged with the other Scottish forces to form Police Scotland. Central Scotland's first Range Rover was probably JLS 979N, dating from March 1975 and inherited from the Stirling & Clackmannan force. Central Scotland then continued to buy Range Rovers until 18th May 1994 when L523 GMS, their last Classic, was registered. The force went on to buy a P38 Range Rover; P112 CMS, registered on 14th April 1997, and an L322; SN53 EOT, a 4.4 litre petrol model which entered service in September 2003. The force then used a number of Discoverys before becoming Police Scotland in 2013.

The early Central Scotland Range Rovers were marked with a red stripe with a force badge and 'Central Scotland Police' on the doors. They were fitted with a large illuminated 'Police' sign and a single blue light and the front of the vehicle was fitted two blue lights and a siren. EMS 896V, which entered service in April 1980, wore the same markings but was fitted with a light bar and two roof mounted searchlights. When C908 YLS entered service in April 1986 it was marked in the same markings as the earlier Range Rovers but at some point in its service, it was re marked in Central Scotland's unique scheme (the same applied to E910 NLS which was also re marked in the new scheme). The scheme consisted of two yellow stripes, bordered in blue, with a force badge and 'Central Scotland Police' on the front doors. When Central Scotland's P38, P112 CMS, entered service in 1997, it was initially marked with a yellow stripe, bordered by blue chequer bands, and the same badge and wording on the front doors (K517 CMS, Central Scotland's penultimate Classic, was also re marked in the new livery). Towards the end of its service, P122 CMS was issued to the force Collision Investigation Unit and re marked in Battenburg with a force badge and 'Central Scotland Police' on the bonnet – Central Scotland's L322 Range Rover was marked in the same way.

Central Scotland's Range Rovers were based on the Traffic Division, patrolling the M9, M80 and M90 motorways and other major roads in the force area.

First Range Rover (probable): JLS 979N (March 1975)

Last Range Rover: SN53 EOT (1st September 2003)

PHOTO 1 – HMS 870S, an early Central Scotland Range Rover, registered on 1st April 1978 (Alan McConnell)

PHOTO 2 – Central Scotland's EMS 896V, shown being driven off road in the Ochil Hills (Alistair Cordiner)

PHOTO 3 – L523 GMS, Central Scotland's last Range Rover Classic, showing the force's unique marking scheme (Jim Burns)

PHOTO 4 – Central Scotland's P38 Range Rover, P122 CMS, shown when it was marked in Battenburg and used by the force Collision Investigation Unit (Alex Watson)

PHOTO 5 – SN53 EOT, Central Scotland's L322 Range Rover (Alan Matthews collection)

Fife Constabulary

The Fife Constabulary was one of only two Scottish forces not to undergo dramatic change in April 1975 (Dumfries & Galloway was the other) and remained unchanged until 1st April 2013 when the force was merged with the other Scottish forces to form Police Scotland. The earliest known Fife Range Rover is USP 982L which was registered on 10th November 1972. Although Fife was never a big user of Range Rovers, the force continued to buy them until October 1991 when J351 ESL entered service. When this last Range Rover was sold in 1994, Fife used a number of Discoverys and Volvo XC70 four-wheel drive estate cars before buying BMW X5s for the Roads Policing and ARV roles.

The earliest recorded Fife Range Rover was marked with a red stripe and 'Police' on the doors and bonnet. The vehicle was fitted with a single blue light and two roof mounted searchlights. By the time B905 WSN entered service in January 1985, the red stripe remained but a force badge and 'Fife Constabulary' had been added to the front doors and the vehicle was fitted with a light bar and two large blue lights on the radiator grille – Fife's last Range Rover was marked in the same scheme.

Fife's Range Rovers were based on the Traffic Division, patrolling the M90 motorway and other major roads in the force area.

First Range Rover: USP 982L (10th November 1972)

Last Range Rover: J351 ESL (1st October 1991)

PHOTO 1 – A rare photograph of USP 982L, Fife's earliest recorded Range Rover (Alan Matthews collection)

PHOTO 2 – Fife's B905 WSN, dating from January 1985 (Bill Greig)

PHOTO 3 – J351 ESL, Fife's last Range Rover (Jim Burns)

Grampian Police

The Grampian Police was formed on 16th May 1975 from the Aberdeen City Police and most of the Scottish North Eastern Counties Constabulary force area. The force was in existence until 1st April 2013 when it was merged with the other Scottish forces to form Police Scotland. Grampian's first Range Rover was HRS 414V which entered service in February 1980 and the force continued to buy Range Rovers (usually one a year) until 18th January 1995 when M699 RSS, their last Classic, was registered. Grampian bought only one P38 Range Rover but then bought three 3.0 litre diesel L322s in 2004 (they were used as ARVs), before buying Discoverys and Volvo XC70 four-wheel drive estate cars.

The first Grampian Range Rover was marked with a thin red stripe and fitted with a large roof mounted 'Police' sign with a single blue light and two roof mounted searchlights. Unusually for a force other than Cheshire, GMP and Lancashire, the bonnet was painted black and fitted with an illuminated 'Police Stop' sign. Apart from a modern light bar and a white bonnet A461 ESO, which entered service in November 1983, was marked in the same way. By the time C611 YST entered service in December 1985, a force badge and 'Grampian Police' had been added to the front doors, and blue reflective tape bordered the red stripe by the time D205 EAS joined the force in December 1986. G588 OSO and H738 URS were both marked with a red stripe along the centre of their sides and reflective chequer bands bordering it were added during at some point in their service. Grampian's P38 and L322 Range Rovers were all marked in Battenburg (the L322s had a force badge and 'Grampian Police' on the bonnet).

Grampian's Range Rovers were largely based on the Traffic Division, patrolling the major roads in the force area. These included the A90 and the A93, both often prone to severe weather in the winter; Range Rovers were the only viable patrol vehicles in these conditions. The Grampian force area included Royal Deeside, the location of a number of royal residences including Balmoral Castle and Birkhall. The area is popular with the royal family, with many members spending the summer months there, and many Grampian officers were deployed on royal duties. Grampian's Range Rovers were used for protection duties and for patrolling the royal estates and the force operated a policy of using unmarked new Range Rovers for royal duties and then marking them for use by Traffic.

First Range Rover: HRS 414V (February 1980)

Last Range Rover: SV54 BPE (11th October 2004)

PHOTO 1 – The only known photograph of HRS 414V, Grampian's first Range Rover, seen escorting an Abnormal Load in Aberdeen (Alan Matthews collection)

PHOTO 2 – Grampian's A461 ESO, registered on 1st November 1983 (Alan Matthews collection)

PHOTO 3 – Grampian's H738 URS, which entered service in January 1991, escorting two large Abnormal Loads (Steve Pearson)

PHOTO 4 – L104 LSA, Grampian's penultimate Range Rover Classic which was registered on 1st November 1993. It is shown at the Nelson Street Traffic garage in Aberdeen (Steve Pearson)

PHOTO 5 – Grampian's P38 Range Rover, V138 DSA, which entered service in November 1999 (Steve Pearson)

PHOTO 6 – SV54 BOU, one of Grampian's three L322 Range Rovers (Alex Watson)

Lothian & Borders Police

The Lothian & Borders Police was formed on 16th May 1975 from the Berwick, Roxburgh & Selkirk Constabulary, the Edinburgh City Police and the Lothian & Peebles Constabulary. On 1st April 2013, Lothian & Borders was merged with the other Scottish forces to form Police Scotland. As far as can be ascertained, two of Lothian & Borders' pre amalgamation forces used Range Rovers: Lothian & Peebles who had MSY 979K (the first Scottish Police Range Rover, registered on 2nd December 1971), RSY 143L (registered in April 1973) and TSY 142M (registered on 8th March 1974) and Edinburgh City who had CSG 114L (registered on 9th March 1973). Two of the pre amalgamation force Range Rovers were transferred to the new force in May 1975 and the first Lothian & Borders Range Rover was almost certainly TSX 49R, registered on 14th September 1976. The force then continued to buy Range Rovers until March 1993 when K705 FSH, their last Classic, entered service. Lothian & Borders decided to buy Tdi Discoverys to replace the Range Rovers (they had also previously bought some Mercedes G Wagens), but in 1996 one of the Discoverys was written off and replaced by Lothian & Borders' first P38 Range Rover, P814 LSX, which was registered on 17th September 1996. Further purchases of P38s followed and the force went on to buy one L322 Range Rover, SK04 AHA (a 3.0 litre diesel model), before buying Discoverys and Volvo XC70 four-wheel drive estate cars.

The Range Rovers used by Lothian & Borders' constituent forces were typical of the early 1970s, being marked with a red stripe and fitted with a roof mounted illuminated 'Police' sign and a single blue light. When TKS 314T entered service in December 1978, the markings were the same with the addition of 'Police' on the doors above the red stripe and the roof mounted 'Police' sign being mounted on a roof bar (which also had two blue lights at each end). Many forces changed from red to yellow stripes in the mid 1980s and Lothian & Borders was one of them. D769 CSC was registered on 1st October 1986 and was marked with a yellow stripe, bordered in reflective blue tape, and a force badge encircled by 'Lothian & Borders Police' on the front doors. The roof lights were the same as previously fitted and E114 LSF, registered on 1st January 1988, was probably the first Lothian & Borders Range Rover to be fitted with a light bar. The force changed their markings again when H869 LFS and H965 LFS entered service in September 1990. The yellow stripe, force badge and logo remained but above the yellow stripe the vehicle was marked with diagonal blue reflective lines, making a very effective scheme. Lothian & Borders' last Classics were marked in the same way (and fitted with Woodway Hy Lights) but the first P38 was marked with blue and yellow diagonal stripes (similar to the Tiger Stripe markings used by West Mercia and West Midlands) and reflective blue and silver chequer bands along the bottom of the doors. The later P38s and the L322 were marked in Battenburg; the L322, SK04 AHA, was marked in Battenburg on a silver vehicle.

The Lothian & Borders Range Rovers were based on the Traffic Division, patrolling the M8 and M9 motorways, the A1, the A7, the A90 and other major roads in the force area; these included the A720 Edinburgh Bypass, one of the most important main roads in Scotland. The Traffic Division HQ, known as the Traffic Link, was based at Force Headquarters at Fettes Avenue, Edinburgh and covered the city and the bypass. Other Traffic garages were at Dalkeith, covering East and Midlothian, Bathgate, covering Westlothian and the M8 and M9 motorways (this garage subsequently moved to nearby Livingston) and Hawick in the Borders area.

First Range Rover: MSY 979K (2nd December 1971)

Last Range Rover: SK04 AHA (July / August 2004)

PHOTO 1 – PC Ian Dalling with MSY 979K, callsign Zulu Golf 12, Lothian & Peebles' first Range Rover (and the first Scottish Police Range Rover). They are shown on patrol on the M8 motorway near Newbridge (Ian Dalling via David Black)

PHOTO 2 – RSY 143L, one of the Lothian & Peebles Range Rovers (Alan McConnell)

PHOTO 3 – A rare photograph of Lothian & Peebles' TSY 142M, seen at Musselburgh in July 1974 (Author's collection)

PHOTO 4 – Lothian & Borders' TKS 314T, callsign Tango 14, dating from December 1978 (Alan McConnell)

PHOTO 5 – E114 LSF, showing the revised Lothian & Borders markings. The extended door mirror was fitted when the vehicle was towing the force caravan (Alan McConnell)

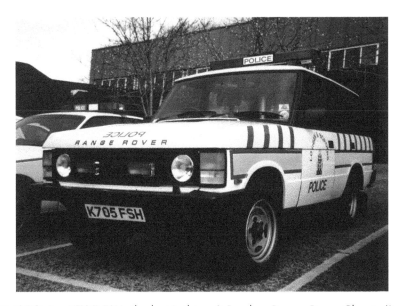

PHOTO 6 – K705 FSH, the last Lothian & Borders Range Rover Classic (Jim Burns)

PHOTO 7 – Lothian & Borders' first P38 Range Rover, P814 LSX; it was also the first Scottish Police P38. The vehicle was based on the Edinburgh Traffic Unit with the callsign of Sierra Tango 14. It was replaced in late 2000 by X649 UMS and then issued to the force Marine Unit (Alan McConnell)

PHOTO 8 – X649 UMS, Lothian & Borders' last P38, registered on 1st December 2000 (Alex Watson)

PHOTO 9 – Lothian & Borders' only L322 Range Rover, SK04 AHA, callsign Sierra Tango 14 (Alex Watson)

Northern Constabulary

The Northern Constabulary was formed on 16th May 1975 from the Inverness Constabulary, the old Northern Constabulary, the Ross & Sutherland Constabulary and parts of the Argyll County Police and Scottish North East Counties Constabulary force areas. It was the Police force covering the largest geographical area in the UK (equivalent to the size of Belgium), but was one of the smallest in terms of officer numbers. The force was in existence until 1st April 2013 when it was merged with the other Scottish forces to form Police Scotland. The first 'NorCon' Range Rovers were WAS 751V and WAS 753V, both registered on 21st November 1979 (WAS 752V may have been another, but it is recorded as being a Rover 2600 car). The force did not buy many more Range Rovers; XST 300V was one, dating from May 1980, and the last three (B308 UST to B310 UST) were registered in December 1984. NorCon then went on to buy a number of different vehicles; four

Mercedes G Wagens were purchased in September 1988, followed by another in 1990 and at least one Ford Maverick in November 1996. The force then returned to Range Rovers, buying V136 LOB, an ex-Land Rover demonstrator 4.0 litre petrol P38 model, in early 2001. In March 2005, although using Discoverys and a 2004 registered BMW X5, NorCon bought their last two Range Rovers; SY05 BAO, a 4.4 litre petrol model and SY05 BAU, a 3.0 litre diesel model. SY05 BAU was subsequently deployed to the force Collision Investigation Unit based at Dingwall and was sold in early 2013, making it the last marked Police Range Rover in Scotland.

The first NorCon Range Rover was marked with a narrow red stripe and a round force badge on the doors. It was fitted with two roof bars on which were mounted an illuminated 'Police' sign, two blue lights and two horns; two spot lights were fitted to the front bumper. XST 300V was marked in the same way but was one of the earlier Police Range Rovers to be fitted with a light bar. The last Classics were marked in the same way but whilst B310 UST was fitted with a light bar, B308 UST was fitted with the same roof bar arrangement as that fitted to the first Range Rovers; it was probably swapped onto the new vehicle when they were sold. NorCon's P38 was marked with a yellow stripe and the updated NorCon badge and logo 'Protect and Serve – Dion is Cuidich' (English and Gaelic) on the front doors; it was also fitted with two light bars and the Premier Hazard Nightscan lighting system. The NorCon L322s were both marked in Battenburg with the force badge and logo on the front doors.

The Northern Constabulary force area contained some of the most stunning scenery in the UK, scenery that is often prone to the severest weather conditions in the winter. The NorCon Range Rovers were bought as a result of a Home Office directive that Police four-wheel drive vehicles should be permanently based at strategic locations in the force area. The Range Rovers were based on the Traffic Division, patrolling the major roads of the Scottish Highlands, including the A9 and the A82.

First Range Rover: WAS 751V (21st November 1979)

Last Range Rover: SY05 BAU (24th March 2005)

PHOTO 1 – Two of Northern Constabulary's first Range Rovers, shown when they were new at Force Headquarters, Old Perth Road, Inverness. The emergency equipment included snowshoes, thick woollen socks and ration packs. The officers are, from left to right: PC Murdo Sutherland, Chief Inspector Dan Green and PC Jimmy Sutherland (Dave Conner / NorCon Museum)

PHOTO 2 – Northern Constabulary's WAS 753V, showing the force badge which had not been added when the first photograph was taken (Steve Pearson)

PHOTO 3 – Northern Constabulary's XST 300V, on patrol in the Lochaber area of the Scottish Highlands in 1982 (Dave Conner / NorCon Museum)

PHOTO 4 – PC David Sutherland and B308 UST (callsign Tango 24), one of the last three Northern Constabulary Range Rover Classics, registered on 1st December 1984. The vehicle was based at Brora, on Scotland's east coast (Dave Conner / NorCon Museum)

PHOTO 5 – PC Obrie and B310 UST on patrol in the Scottish Highlands (S.J. Obrie)

PHOTO 6 – Northern Constabulary's P38 Range Rover, V136 LOB. Bought from Land Rover in early 2001, it was still in service in 2005 (Dave Conner)

PHOTO 7 – SY05 BAO, one of Northern Constabulary's last two Range Rovers, photographed in May 2009 (Dave Conner)

Strathclyde Police

Strathclyde was the largest Scottish Police force and was formed on 16th May 1975 from six smaller forces: the Ayrshire Constabulary, the City of Glasgow Police, the Dunbartonshire Constabulary, the Lanarkshire Constabulary, the Renfrew & Bute Constabulary and parts of the Argyll County Police and the Stirling & Clackmannan Constabulary force areas. The force was in existence until 1st April 2013 when it was merged with the other Scottish forces to form Police Scotland.

At least four of Strathclyde's constituent forces used Range Rovers. The City of Glasgow had CGE 884K and CGE 885K, registered in January 1972 and Ayrshire was next, registering four Range Rovers, XSD 337L to XSD 340L in August and September 1972 and another two (RAG 76M and RAG 77M) on 2nd May 1974. Lanarkshire bought two Range Rovers before amalgamation: LVA 962L, registered in February 1973, and JGB 671N, registered in

March 1975, just two months prior to amalgamation. The most interesting Scottish pre amalgamation Range Rover was TSB 695L, used by the Argyll County Police in the northernmost part of what became the Strathclyde force area, and their Range Rover was almost unique in UK Police service. Very few marked UK Police Range Rovers were anything other than Davos White but Argyll County's, registered on 9th July 1973, was Tuscan Blue, the colour being chosen so that it would stand out in the snow when it was being used by the Mountain Rescue Team. The vehicle was based at Glencoe Police Station which was taken over by the Northern Constabulary in 1975. It was then the subject of a successful (if somewhat acrimonious) merger bid by Strathclyde and was deployed to the Strathclyde Traffic garage at Dumbarton, on the A82 north west of Glasgow. The first Range Rovers bought by Strathclyde were NYS 487P and NYS 488P, registered on 1st March 1976 (almost certainly replacing the two K registered City of Glasgow vehicles). The force then maintained a fleet of Range Rovers until April 1988 when their last two Classics, E207 BGB and E208 BGB, were registered.

Strathclyde was one several forces which saw the launch of the Discovery in 1989 as a way of saving money and the force was joint first (with Dyfed-Powys) to buy the new vehicle. Strathclyde's first Discovery, H348 FAC (one of their three V8is), was supplied to the force by Land Rover on a 'try / buy' arrangement and further purchases followed in January 1991 (V8is), late 1992 / early 1993 (200Tdis) and late 1994 (300 Tdis). A few Strathclyde Range Rovers were kept in service, however, including E104 XGD which, having seen service on the Motherwell Motorway Unit, was fitted with a Tdi diesel engine and issued to the Mounted Branch. Another survivor was the last Classic, E208 BGB which, following service on the Glasgow Motorway Unit, was issued to the Argyll Traffic Unit at Lochgilphead. The vehicle was written off in January 1995 when it left the road during heavy snowfall and crashed into a loch; fortunately, the driver escaped unharmed.

Strathclyde's purchase of Discoverys was, in common with other forces which bought Tdi Discoverys for motorway work, almost universally unpopular with the officers that used them. It was for this reason that when the last three Classic demonstrators became available, Strathclyde bought them all (in March / April 1996). The vehicles were L470 YAC (3.9 litre petrol, fitted with an automatic gearbox and Electronic Air Suspension), M583 CVC and M584 CVC (both 3.9 petrol, fitted with the R380 manual gearbox). The force made good use of the last Classics; M584 CVC, for example, was used by the Motherwell Motorway Unit before being replaced, along with the other ex-demonstrators, by a Discovery II Td5 in March 2000. On 1st December 1997, Strathclyde registered their first two P38 Range Rovers, R647 PSB and R653 PSB; they were both 4.0 litre petrol models. Only two more purchases followed; R654 PSB in February 1998 and T481 ASB in June 1999 (again, both 4.0 litre petrol models) and the force then bought a number of different vehicles for the Traffic patrol role. These included Mercedes ML320s, ML270s, Mitsubishi Shoguns and BMW X5s. The Strathclyde Range Rover story did not quite end with the last P38, however, as the force bought the partially armoured P38, P628 WNL, from Durham on 17th August 2001.

Strathclyde's markings changed very little over the years and the City of Glasgow Range Rovers were marked in a scheme very similar to those used on the last Strathclyde Classics over twenty five years later. The markings consisted of a red stripe with the force badge and 'Strathclyde Police' on the front doors. Ayrshire's XSD 337L was initially unmarked (but fitted with a large illuminated 'Police' sign and a single blue light and a 'Police' sign on the radiator grille). The vehicle was subsequently marked with a red stripe with 'Police' above the stripe on the doors. Lanarkshire's second Range Rover, JGB 671N, was marked with a red stripe with the force badge and 'Police' on the doors. The roof of the vehicle was fitted with a large illuminated 'Police' sign, topped by two horns, with blue lights either side of it; two searchlights were also fitted on the roof. Strathclyde's P38 Range Rovers were all marked in Battenburg.

Strathclyde's Range Rovers were largely based on the Traffic Division with Motorway Units at Glasgow and Motherwell and other units based at locations including Argyll and Dumbarton. The force area was considerable and included a large amount of motorway and main road mileage, much of it prone to severe weather conditions in the winter. The motorways included the M8 as far east as Harthill Services, the M73, the M74 / A74(M) as far south as Harthope Viaduct near Moffat and the M80. Strathclyde's main roads included the A82 and A83 in Argyll; both beautiful in the summer but treacherous in the winter. Strathclyde made good use of their Range Rovers and many were issued to other units following Motorway or Traffic use. The Mounted Branch and the Tactical Firearms Unit were among the units to use ex-Traffic, and generally unmarked, Range Rovers.

First Range Rover: CGE 884K (January 1972)

Last Range Rover: T481 ASB (1st June 1999)

PHOTO 1 – The only known photograph of the City of Glasgow's CGE 884K. The vehicle is shown with its crew and equipment (via Paul Miller)

PHOTO 2 – Ayrshire Constabulary's first Range Rover, XSD 337L, photographed near Prestwick Airport. The vehicle was based on the Ayrshire Traffic Department at Ayr and other Ayrshire Range Rovers were based at Irvine and Kilmarnock (Robert Campbell)

PHOTO 3 – Ayrshire's XSD 337L parked next to a 1930 4.5 litre Bentley Le Mans replica (via Jim Burns)

PHOTO 4 – Argyll County Police's Tuscan Blue Range Rover, TSB 695L, photographed at Glencoe after amalgamation in 1975 but still in Argyll County markings. The two officers are PC Nigel Stafford (left) and the late PC John Allen (right) (Nigel Stafford via Dave Conner)

PHOTO 5 – Lanarkshire's second Range Rover, JGB 671N, dating from March 1975. The vehicle was based at Motherwell, patrolling the A74, and was transferred to Strathclyde when the force was formed in May 1975, remaining at Motherwell (via Paul Miller)

PHOTO 6 – NYS 488P, one of Strathclyde's first Range Rovers, shown in a force recruiting advert (via Paul Miller)

PHOTO 7 – Strathclyde's NYS 488P towing the force Underwater Search Unit's trailer. The unit used the Range Rover after their new R registration Land Rover 109 Station Wagon was destroyed by fire (via Paul Miller)

PHOTO 8 – NGE 698V, one of a number of Strathclyde Range Rovers registered on 1st February 1980. The vehicle was based at Motherwell (via Paul Miller)

PHOTO 9 – E208 BGD, Strathclyde's last 'new' Range Rover Classic, registered on 24th April 1988. It is shown at Lochgilphead, Argyll, in October 1994 having 'retired' from the Glasgow Motorway Unit (Paul Miller)

PHOTO 10 – L470 YAC, one of the last three Police Range Rover demonstrators, bought by Strathclyde in 1996. The vehicle was based on the Glasgow Motorway Unit (Geraint Roberts)

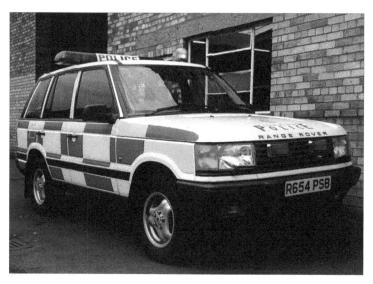

PHOTO 11 – Strathclyde's third P38 Range Rover, R654 PSB, registered on 1st February 1998. The vehicle was based on the Glasgow Motorway Unit (Jim Burns)

Tayside Police

Tayside Police was formed on 16th May 1975 from the Angus Constabulary, the Dundee City Police and part of the Perth & Kinross Constabulary force area. The force was in existence until 1st April 2013 when it was merged with the other Scottish forces to form Police Scotland. The earliest Tayside Range Rover was Dundee City's TYJ 12M, registered in September 1973. The force then continued to buy Range Rovers until December 1994 when L345 SSL entered service. Having been the second force in Scotland to buy the Discovery, Tayside bought a number of them when the last Range Rovers were sold. Other vehicles used by Tayside included Vauxhall Montereys, Mercedes ML320s and ML350s Mitsubishi Shoguns and Toyota Landcruisers. In January 2003, when ST52 HBA entered service, Tayside became the first Scottish force to buy the BMW X5. Unusually though, the vehicle was not a great success and no further purchases followed.

Although the last Tayside Range Rover was a 3.9 litre petrol model, the force had previously carried out some interesting conversion work on one of their older Range Rovers. Concerned about rising fuel costs, Tayside contacted a Land Rover specialist in Scotland and had one of the older Range Rovers (possibly D354 FSN) converted to diesel using a 3.5 litre Mazda engine; a popular conversion at the time. News of this work reached Land Rover who then used two Tayside Range Rovers, G475 USL and H545 YSR, as prototypes for the Tdi retro fit conversion.

Dundee City's TYJ 12M was simply marked with a red stripe and fitted with a small illuminated 'Police' sign and single blue light. At some stage in its service the roof sign was replaced by a much larger sign with loud speakers fitted at each end of it. By the time TSR 683S entered service in April 1978, 'Tayside Police' and a force badge had been added to the doors, the roof sign had been replaced by a single blue light and the vehicle was fitted with two blue lights and a siren on the front bumper. Although light bars were fitted from the early / mid 1980s, Tayside's markings remained almost unchanged until the early / mid 1990s when a new scheme was introduced. The first Tdi retro fit, G475 USL, was re marked in the new scheme which consisted of a red stripe, bordered along the top by chequer bands and larger chequer bands along the door bottoms. A small force badge and 'Tayside Police' was on the front doors and 'Police' in reflective blue lettering was on the rear wings. L345 SSL, Tayside's last Range Rover, was the first Scottish Range Rover to be marked in Battenburg but the force, in common with many others, did not adopt the new scheme. L345 SSL was subsequently re marked in a slight variation of the force markings; the red stripe was wider, the force badge was moved to the rear wings and 'Tayside Police' was on the front doors. The vehicle did, however retain remnants of the Battenburg scheme; a red reflective stripe along the roof, silver reflective material on the windscreen pillar and blue reflective material on the door pillars. At least one of Tayside's Divisional Range Rovers was fitted with a half width Premier Hazard Minimax light bar, as opposed to the full width version fitted to the Traffic vehicles.

Although some Tayside Range Rovers were used on Divisions, most of them were based on the Traffic Division, patrolling the M90 motorway, the A9 and other major roads in the force area

First Range Rover: TYJ 12M (September 1973)

Last Range Rover: L345 SSL (31st December 1994)

PHOTO 1 – Dundee City's TYJ 12M, registered in September 1973 (Alan Matthews collection)

PHOTO 2 – TYJ 12M with the larger roof sign, fitted later its service (Alan Matthews collection)

PHOTO 3 – Tayside's TSR 683S, registered on 1st April 1978, shown just off the M90 motorway (although this part was designated as the M85 at the time). The bridge is Friarton Bridge spanning the River Tay, the Dundee to Perth railway line and the A85 (Tayside Police)

PHOTO 4 – E235 HTS, dating from October 1987, showing the Tayside markings used from the 1980s to the 1990s (Alan Matthews collection)

PHOTO 5 – The first Tayside Tdi retro fit, G475 USL, shown in the updated force markings at Kinross Police Station (Paul Miller)

PHOTO 6 – L345 SSL, callsign Whiskey Tango 45, Tayside's last Range Rover and the first in Scotland to be marked in Battenburg (Paul Miller)

Royal Ulster Constabulary & Police Service of Northern Ireland

The Royal Ulster Constabulary (RUC) was the Police force for Northern Ireland from 1922 to 2001. It was in existence throughout the violent conflict known as 'The Troubles' and 302 of its members were killed in the line of duty. The bravery of the RUC throughout 'The Troubles' resulted in the award to the force of the George Cross by Her Majesty the Queen on 23rd November 1999. On 4th November 2001 the RUC was reformed and renamed, becoming the Police Service of Northern Ireland (PSNI).

The first RUC Range Rover was EOI 6912 which entered service in September 1972. The vehicle, which cost £2335.78, was the first of twenty RUC Range Rovers, the last being SOI 5639 which arrived on 25th October 1977. The last Range Rover in use was POI 8616 which was withdrawn from use on 2nd June 1986. Having not used Range Rovers for over ten years, the RUC bought least four P38 Range Rovers (the first was probably ECZ 3053 which entered service on 6th October 2000) and the PSNI bought ten L322s with the first, UCZ 7324, entering service on 5th

April 2004. The PSNI's last Range Rover in service was FEZ 8142 (based at Castlereagh) and by the time this was sold on 9th September 2019, the force was using Mitsubishi Shoguns, having previously also used Discoverys and Vauxhall Montereys.

The twenty early RUC Range Rovers were almost unique among those used by UK Police forces in that they were unmarked and only one of them was white. The remaining nineteen were painted in the standard Range Rover colours of the 1970s: Tuscan Blue (7), Sahara Dust (6), Bahama Gold (3), Masai Red (2) and Lincoln Green (1). Although unmarked, the RUC Range Rovers were fitted with a magnetic 'Police' sign and single blue light and a Findlay Irvine 'Icelert' warning device under the front bumper. They were also equipped with 'Makrolon' plastic ballistic protection to varying degrees. The later vehicles were fitted with Makrolon side windows and internal windscreens and the early vehicles were often modified during their service.

The RUC P38 Range Rovers were bought during the transition to the PSNI and, whilst they were marked in Battenburg, they do not appear to have had any force badges and the PSNI badge was added to the rear side windows after November 2001. Unusually, the light bars on some of the P38s were attached to roof rails. The L322s were marked in Battenburg on silver vehicles, with 'Police' in large reflective letters along the door bottoms and a force badge on the bonnet and rear side windows; they were also fitted with the Premier Hazard Nightscan lighting system.

The RUC Range Rovers were all initially based on the Traffic Division, patrolling the M1, M2, M12 and M22 motorways from bases at Armagh, Ballyclare, Ballymena and Castlereagh. Later motorways were the M3 and M5 and the PSNI Road Policing Strategic Unit and Road Policing Support Unit Range Rovers were also based at Maydown in County Londonderry, Steeple Road, Antrim and Mahon Road, Portadown.

Some of the early Range Rovers were also used by non-motorway Traffic and a number of Headquarters departments.

First Range Rover: EOI 6912 (19th September 1972)

Last Range Rover: FEZ 8143 (15th August 2006)

PHOTO 1 – The RUC's first female Traffic officers with Bahama Gold Range Rover EOI 7361, callsign Tango 58, circa June 1974. The officers (from left to right) are: WPCs Maureen Long, Janet Millar and Evelyn Penny, Chief Superintendent Jane Gallagher, Inspector Muriel Price, WPCs Pat Millar, Iris Montgomery and Frances Gabbie (James Craig)

PHOTO 2 – WPC Gabbie, shown with EOI 7361 in a publicity photograph taken in 1974 (Fran Milligan)

PHOTO 3 – The RUC 1974 Road Accidents Report showing WPC Gabbie and EOI 7361 and an RUC Tuscan Blue Range Rover on patrol on the M2 motorway (Author's collection)

PHOTO 4 – The RUC's last P38 Range Rover, HCZ 4383, which entered service on 23rd March 2001 (Paul Stokes)

PHOTO 5 – FEZ 8143, the PSNI's last Range Rover, which was disposed of on 7th January 2015. The vehicle was based at Steeple Road, Antrim (Alex Watson)

CHAPTER 6

PRESERVED POLICE RANGE ROVERS

Despite being well driven and well maintained, the lives faced by the majority of Police Range Rovers was hard and it is a testament to the vehicle that any have survived to be preserved for the future. They are all historic vehicles, though, and at least two Range Rovers were sent from Police service into nationally important collections such as the British Motor Museum at Gaydon in Warwickshire and the Dunsfold Collection in Surrey, the world's largest collection of Land Rovers. It is, however, largely due to clubs such as the Police Vehicle Enthusiasts Club and Police Car UK, as well as a number of private individuals, that a growing number of Police Range Rovers have been preserved.

Range Rover Classic

TJA 972X: ex-Greater Manchester Police. The oldest preserved Police Range Rover, TJA 972X was registered on 8th October 1981; one of a batch of thirteen GMP Range Rovers (TJA 961X to TJA 973X) registered between 1st and 8th October 1981. The vehicle was built at Land Rover's Solihull factory on 26th August 1981 and dispatched to Drabble & Allen, the Manchester Land Rover dealer, on 2nd September 1981. Originally destined for GMP's Motorway Group, TJA 972X was instead issued to the force Technical Communications Branch and equipped as a Command Vehicle. It was marked in a different scheme from the Traffic vehicles (a wide black and white chequer band on the sides of the vehicle) and fitted with sophisticated radio equipment. Based at GMP's Headquarters, the Range Rover led an easy life, covering only 47,000 miles in ten years. In 1991 TJA 972X was in danger of being disposed of until Inspector Geoff Taylor of the

Motorway Group had to foresight to use it as part of a Motorway Safety display. The vehicle was marked and equipped as a 1970s GMP Traffic Range Rover and continued in the Road Safety / Public Relations role until 1997 when it was transferred to GMP's force museum. By 2005, TJA 972X was in need of restoration but the museum did have the funds to do it so Geoff Taylor, now retired, bought it at auction, restored it and loaned it back to the museum. Although TJA 972X is no longer on display in the GMP Museum, it is often displayed at public events and has also been used as an escort vehicle at Police funerals.

B289 HAB: ex-West Mercia Constabulary, one a batch of three West Mercia Range Rovers (B288 HAB to B290 HAB) registered on 8th January 1985. The vehicle was in service from January 1985 to March 1988 and was based at Strensham Services on the M5 motorway. The vehicle has been restored by its owner, John Rundle.

E532 LYO: ex-Metropolitan Police, one of a batch of three Met Range Rovers (E531 LYO to E533 LYO) with E532 LYO being registered on 30th July 1988. The vehicle was used by the Met Bomb Squad and was sold on 6th April 2000 with only 48,000 miles recorded. It was restored by Paul Stokes, spent some time in a museum in Italy and is now preserved at the Dunsfold Collection.

F798 FAM: ex-Wiltshire Constabulary, registered on 1st September 1988. The vehicle was restored by Paul Ridley.

L867 SMA: ex-Cheshire Constabulary, one of four Cheshire Tdi Range Rovers (L864 SMA to L867 SMA) registered in July 1994. The vehicle was based at Knutsford Services on the M6 motorway and was Cheshire's last Range Rover Classic. It is currently undergoing restoration by its owner, Steve Rodman.

N760 OYR: ex-Metropolitan Police, registered on 11th January 1996. The vehicle was the Met's last Range Rover Classic and is currently undergoing restoration by its owner, Richard Hopkins.

N673 CUK: ex-West Midlands Police. The vehicle was the last Police Range Rover Classic, being registered on 1st May 1996. It is currently undergoing restoration by West Midlands Police.

P38 Range Rover

M751 CVC: ex-Land Rover and Metropolitan Police, registered on 13th October 1994. The vehicle was the first Police P38 Range Rover demonstrator and was sold to the Met on 19th March 1997. It was issued to the Met Special Escort Group and on 6th September 1997, it escorted the coffin of Diana, Princess of Wales, on its journey from London to Althorp in Northamptonshire. The vehicle was sold by the Met on 13th December 2001 and has been restored by its owner, Richard Hopkins.

M752 CVC: ex-Land Rover and Metropolitan Police, registered on 14th October 1994. The vehicle was one of the early Police P38 Range Rover demonstrators and was sold to the Met on 19th March 1997. The vehicle was sold by the Met on 19th June 2002 and has been restored by its owner, Richard Hopkins.

P83 JOX: ex-West Midlands Police, registered on 1st January 1997. The vehicle was probably West Midlands' first P38 Range Rover and was based on the Central Motorway Police Group. It was sold by West Midlands on 3rd June 2011 having covered 186,000 miles. The vehicle was restored by Paul Ridley and is now owned by Tony Latham.

P628 WNL: ex-Durham Constabulary and Strathclyde Police, registered on 19th February 1997. The vehicle is partially armoured and was sold to Strathclyde on 17th August 2001. It was in service until October 2005 and is now preserved at the British Motor Museum, Gaydon.

P572 ERJ: ex-Greater Manchester Police, registered on 4th March 1997. One of a batch of fourteen GMP Range Rovers registered between 11th September 1996 and 4th March 1997. The vehicle was based at Birch Services on the M62 motorway and allocated to PC X2709 Alec McMurphy. It was restored by Paul Ridley and is now owned by Graham Carter and Jon Smith.

W623 JJA: ex-Greater Manchester Police, registered on 1st August 2000. One of a batch of six GMP Range Rovers (W618 JJA to W623 JJA) registered between 10th July and 1st August 2000. It was preserved and displayed at the GMP Museum but its current status is not known.

GK52 NLA: ex-Kent County Constabulary, one of two Kent Range Rovers (GK52 NLC was the other) registered on 1st September 2002. The vehicle started its service as an Incident Command Vehicle before being allocated to Roads Policing at Coldharbour near Maidstone, with the callsign Tango Delta 42. The vehicle was sold by Kent on 1st July 2010 and has been restored by its owner, Mick Shaw, a retired Derbyshire officer.

L322 Range Rover

DK54 HSU: ex-Cheshire Constabulary, registered on 5th October 2004. The vehicle was Cheshire's last Range Rover and is preserved at the Dunsfold Collection.

PN57 USY: ex-Merseyside Police, registered on 5th December 2007. The vehicle was Merseyside's last Range Rover and was based on the Roads Policing Unit at Maghull, north of Liverpool and near the M57 and M58 motorways. PN57 USY was PC Wayne Hargreaves' posted car and it's callsign was usually Mike Charlie 31. The vehicle was purchased by Paul Ridley in May 2020 and is undergoing restoration.

PHOTO 1 – GMP's TJA 972X as first preserved, with 1970s markings and equipment. (Author's collection)

PHOTO 2 – TJA 972X, preserved in the markings it wore for most of its service (Maurice Kime)

PHOTO 3 – West Mercia's B289 HAB, owned and restored by John Rundle (Ronnie Moore via John Rundle)

PHOTO 4 – Wiltshire's F798 FAM (Paul Ridley)

PHOTO 5 – N760 OYR, the Met's last Range Rover Classic, now owned by Richard Hopkins and under restoration (Richard Hopkins)

PHOTO 6 – The Met's M751 CVC, one of the pair of ex-Met P38 Range Rovers owned by Richard Hopkins (Richard Hopkins)

PHOTO 7 – West Midlands' P83 JOX, restored by Paul Ridley and now owned by Tony Latham (Maurice Kime via Paul Ridley)

PHOTO 8 – P628 WNL, the ex-Durham and Strathclyde partially armoured P38 Range Rover, preserved at the British Motor Museum, Gaydon (Steve Pearson)

PHOTO 9 – GMP's P572 ERJ, restored by Paul Ridley and now owned by Graham Carter and Jon Smith (Paul Ridley)

PHOTO 10 – Kent's GK52 NLA at its first post restoration show at Ashbourne, Derbyshire, in September 2019 (Mick Shaw)

PHOTO 11 – DK54 HSU, Cheshire's last Range Rover, preserved at the Dunsfold Collection (Iain Kitchen)

PHOTO 12 – Merseyside's last Range Rover, PN57 USY, now owned by Paul Ridley and under restoration (Paul Ridley)

Lightning Source UK Ltd.
Milton Keynes UK
UKHW020217101120
373078UK00007B/343

9 781839 752711